SUSTAINABLE INVESTING

SUSTAINABLE INVESTING

WHAT EVERYONE NEEDS TO KNOW®

H. KENT BAKER,
HUNTER M. HOLZHAUER,
AND
JOHN R. NOFSINGER

OXFORD
UNIVERSITY PRESS

OXFORD
UNIVERSITY PRESS

Oxford University Press is a department of the University of Oxford.
It furthers the University's objective of excellence in research, scholarship,
and education by publishing worldwide. Oxford is a registered trade mark of
Oxford University Press in the UK and certain other countries.

"What Everyone Needs to Know" is a registered trademark of
Oxford University Press.

Published in the United States of America by Oxford University Press
198 Madison Avenue, New York, NY 10016, United States of America.

Library of Congress Cataloging-in-Publication Data
Names: Baker, H. Kent (Harold Kent), 1944- author. |
Holzhauer, Hunter M., author. | Nofsinger, John R., author.
Title: Sustainable investing / H. Kent Baker, Hunter M. Holzhauer,
and John R. Nofsinger.
Description: New York, NY : Oxford University Press, [2022] |
Series: What everyone needs to know | Includes index.
Identifiers: LCCN 2021057784 (print) | LCCN 2021057785 (ebook) |
ISBN 9780197643785 (paperback) | ISBN 9780197643815 (hardback) |
ISBN 9780197643808 (epub)
Subjects: LCSH: Investments—Moral and ethical aspects. |
Impact investing | Investments—Social aspects.
Classification: LCC HG4515.13 .B36 2022 (print) |
LCC HG4515.13 (ebook) | DDC 174/.4—dc23/eng/20211202
LC record available at https://lccn.loc.gov/2021057784
LC ebook record available at https://lccn.loc.gov/2021057785

DOI: 10.1093/oso/9780197643815.001.0001

1 3 5 7 9 8 6 4 2

Paperback printed by LSC Communications, United States of America
Hardback printed by Bridgeport National Bindery, Inc., United States of America

CONTENTS

2. Corporate Social Responsibility: Delivering Both Profit and Purpose   34

3. Social and Religious Values: Aligning Values and Portfolio Assets   65

5. Performance Implications of Sustainable Investing: Can You Have Your Cake and Eat It Too?   139

6. Building a Portfolio with a Purpose: How to Benefit You and Society   174

WHY DID WE WRITE THIS BOOK?

We are longtime friends and have worked together on various books and research projects. Additionally, we have a deep interest in sustainable investing and view it as a wave of the future. Given the dynamic pace of sustainable investing, it's unsurprising that various books examine different facets of sustainability, ranging from textbooks to specialized topics such as investing in renewable energy and affordable housing. These books also focus on different audiences like institutional and other professional investors, individual investors, companies, and academics.

Given both the breadth and depth of this sprawling field, this relatively short book is not all-encompassing. Trying to cover everything for all potential audiences is unrealistic. Therefore, our book focuses on helping individual investors understand sustainable investing's leading issues and how they can become sustainable investors. Although some other books target individual investors, we believe a gap exists in treating the subject and covering underlying topics. Thus, we use a question-and-answer (Q&A) format to examine some of sustainable investing's most critical questions in a concise and user-friendly manner. The design enables you to browse for topics of interest if you choose not to read the book from cover to cover. Furthermore, each chapter contains insightful and amusing quotes, highlighted in boxes that create interest and relate to specific questions. These quotes come from noted investment professionals and others.

Sustainable Investing: What Everyone Needs to Know tries to demystify sustainable investing for individual investors who might be interested in adding such investments to their portfolios. It attempts to identify what everyone needs to know about sustainable investing and what they want to know about this fascinating subject. The book also offers a balanced explanation of the broad issues associated with sustainable investing concisely but authoritatively. However, you'll need to determine whether the book accomplishes its goals.

WHOM DO WE WANT TO THANK?

John Maxwell, an American clergyman, once said, "Teamwork makes the dream work." This statement applies to the writing and publishing of this book. With three authors, the sum is greater than the parts because each author makes unique contributions to achieve a common goal. Hence, the book is a team effort in which the team accomplishes more than anyone could achieve independently. However, much more goes into publishing a book.

Although many people played an essential role in this process, we want to single out a few. First, we thank the anonymous reviewers of our book proposal for their helpful comments about the most relevant topics to include in the book. Second, we greatly appreciate the highly professional work done by all our partners at Oxford University Press. In particular, we recognize the contributions of James Cook (Editor) and Macey Fairchild (Assistant Editor), who helped to move the book through the process. Additionally, Kopu Koperundevi (Project Manager) from Newgen Knowledge Works did an excellent job guiding the book through the production process. Third, we appreciate the support provided by our respective institutions: the Kogod School of Business at American University, Rollins College of Business at the University of Tennessee at Chattanooga, and College of Business and Public Policy, University of Alaska, Anchorage. Finally, we thank our families and dedicate this book to them: Linda and Rory Baker, Anna Nofsinger, and Mikael Holzhauer.

WHO ARE THE AUTHORS?

H. Kent Baker, CFA, CMA, is a University Professor of Finance in the Kogod School of Business at American University, Washington, DC. Professor Baker is among the top 1% of the most prolific authors in finance. For example, he is an award-winning author/editor who has published 40 books, including *Socially Responsible Finance and Investing: Financial Institutions, Corporations, Investors, and Activists* (John Wiley & Sons). Professor Baker has also published 200 peer-reviewed journal articles and more than 160 other articles, monographs, book chapters, and proceedings. His research appears in the *Journal of Finance, Journal of Financial and Quantitative Analysis, Financial Management, Journal of Corporate Finance, Journal of Futures Markets, Financial Analysts Journal, Journal of Portfolio Management,* and *Harvard Business Review,* among many others. In addition, he serves on 13 editorial/advisory boards and is the editor of the H. Kent Baker Investments Series at Emerald Publishing. Professor Baker is internationally known for his work in behavioral finance, survey research, and dividend policy. He has consulting and training experience with more than 100 organizations in the United States, Canada, and Europe. He has received numerous research, teaching, and service awards, including the American University's Scholar/ Teacher of the Year and Southern Finance Association's 2019 Distinguished Scholar. Professor Baker has a BSBA (management) from Georgetown University; an MBA (finance), MEd (educational administration), and DBA (finance) from the University of Maryland; and an MS (quantitative methods), MA (training and career development), PhD (educational administration and organizational development), and PhD (counseling and student development) from American University. He is also a professional musician who plays five instruments and has recorded and toured.

Hunter M. Holzhauer is the Robert L. Maclellan and UC Foundation Associate Professor of Finance in the Rollins College of Business at the University of Tennessee at Chattanooga. Professor Holzhauer is an award-winning professor in research, teaching, and service. Since 2013, he has published 16 peer-reviewed articles and authored seven book chapters on socially responsible investing, behavioral finance, and alternative investments. Professor Holzhauer has published in the *Social Responsibility Journal, Journal of Investing, Journal of Applied Finance, Journal of Risk Finance,* and *Journal of Behavioral and Experimental Finance.* He teaches investments, financial analysis, portfolio management, and behavioral finance. Professor Holzhauer also is the creator and Director of the Student Managed Investment Learning Experience (SMILE) Fund and the faculty advisor of two smaller student-managed funds, totaling about $1.5 million in assets under student management. He serves as the faculty advisor for multiple award-winning student investment teams at the regional and global levels. Professor Holzhauer is currently a board member for the Southern Finance Association, an investment committee member for the nonprofit Community Foundation of Greater Chattanooga, and a founding board member for the nonprofit Mario Foundation. He previously was a credit analyst with Colonial Bank and a financial planner and fixed-income portfolio manager with AmSouth Bank. Professor Holzhauer received a BS in business administration and bio-psychology from Birmingham-Southern College, an MBA from Mississippi State University, and a PhD from the University of Alabama.

John R. Nofsinger is a Professor of Finance and Dean of the College of Business and Public Policy at the University of Alaska Anchorage. He is an award-winning book author who has written or edited 15 finance trade books, textbooks, and scholarly books. Professor Nofsinger is a prolific scholar who has published 73 articles in prestigious academic and practitioner journals. His research appears in the *Journal of Finance, Journal of Financial and Quantitative Analysis, Journal of Business, Journal of Business Ethics, Journal of Corporate Finance, Financial Analysts Journal, Financial Management*, and *Journal of Banking and Finance*, among many others. He is most widely known in behavioral finance, socially responsible investing, and the biology of finance. Professor Nofsinger runs Finance ESP: Education Scholarship Practice (financeesp.com). He has been quoted or appeared in the financial media, including *The Wall Street Journal, Financial Times, Fortune, Business Week, Smart Money, Money Magazine, Washington Post, Bloomberg, Nightly Business Report* (NBR), CNBC, and other media from *The Dolans* to *MarketWatch*. Professor Nofsinger has a BSEE from Washington State University, an MBA from Chapman University, and a PhD (finance) from Washington State University. He was a Spartan trifecta obstacle course racer and a five-time Ironman.

WHAT IS THE BOOK ABOUT?

A common assumption about investors is that they're only concerned about making money. They can achieve this goal by optimizing performance. That is, they either want to maximize their future return for a given level of risk or minimize their risk to achieve a specific future return. For some investors, this mindset still rings true. Yet, a growing number of investors challenge this stereotype and would instead prefer to "make money mean more." To many investors, values are important but often forgotten or unrecognized in mainstream finance. Thus, investors frequently have dual goals: making money and doing good. Their goals are both financial and nonfinancial. However, this doesn't necessarily mean that such investors place ethics or values ahead of sound financial decisions.

This emerging viewpoint, called *sustainable investing*, has gained substantial momentum in the last few decades. This book aims to demystify sustainable investing, specifically for "average" investors, and help you navigate the transformation into investing sustainably. It focuses on individual investors, also called retail investors. Sprinkled throughout each chapter are investment quotes. These snapshots of wisdom indicate how investors approach investing, which you can use as learning tools.

Sustainable investing is the process of investing in sustainable companies or funds. It often involves any investment approach that considers environmental, social, and corporate governance (ESG) criteria when selecting and managing investments. However, ESG generally has a stricter definition than sustainable investing. Additionally, what constitutes sustainable investing has a subjective element associated with it.

A landmark study entitled "Who Cares Wins" first coined the term *ESG* in 2004. However, conscience-based investing has a rich history dating back about 3,500 years. In biblical times, Jewish law mandated ethical investing. Likewise, Islam's religious teaching prohibits investing in alcohol, pork, gambling, armaments, and gold and silver. In the United States, the origins of ESG date back to the 18th century, when the Methodists avoided investments in companies manufacturing liquor or tobacco products or promoting gambling. Later, the Quakers forbade investments in slavery and war. Finally, in 1928, a group in Boston founded the first publicly offered investment fund called the Pioneer Fund (now Amundi US), deploying socially responsible investment criteria. These sustainable businesses provide valuable goods and services to society.

Over time, the notion of combining both profit and purpose grew from a fringe idea with few investors to a widespread movement. Sustainability is now mainstream. The terminology evolved to include such labels as "ethical investing," "mission-related investing," "responsible investing," "socially responsible investing," "sustainable investing," "values-based investing," "green investing," "impact investing," and "community investing," depending on the emphasis. This book consolidates all of these efforts under the generic term "sustainable investing." Since the 1960s, this form of investing has gained momentum and has developed into a consistent philosophy. In the 1980s, it was mainly about what investors didn't want to own. In other words, they shunned or excluded investments in certain types of companies and industries. Since the 1990s, investors have increasingly focused on investing for the greater good of society. Today, many investors demand that their investments generate returns and have a positive impact on the world. As a result, sustainability considerations are becoming an increasingly important part of their investment considerations. In summary, the tectonic shift toward sustainable investing is accelerating.

Although the underlying idea of doing well financially while doing good for society has been around for centuries, sustainable investing's scope has expanded to include social change. Instead of screening out investments in "sin" industries like alcohol, gambling, tobacco, and weapons, sustainable investing has evolved to make investments in organizations that create a positive impact. The growing demand for such assets has come about mainly due to a changing investor profile. Many of today's investors view an investment's value as more than just earning a return and building one's nest egg. Although firms often market sustainable investing to millennials and women, it attracts widespread interest. Investors also want their investments to reflect their social values and positively impact society and the world.

Today, ESG-responsible corporations go beyond *corporate social responsibility* (CSR), referring to their efforts to affect stakeholders. CSR companies treat their customers, employees, suppliers, and communities well, create healthy products and services, avoid unethical or predatory business practices, and exhibit moral leadership involving shareholder rights, executive pay, and internal controls.

As with any investment, sustainable investing has both pros and cons. On the positive side, you get to experience the feeling that your assets support your beliefs and values. It lets you "put your money where your mouth is." By taking a stand, you're showing that you mean what you say instead of just talking about it. In colloquial terms, you're "talking the talk" and "walking the walk." You may also feel you're enacting change and supporting companies that you view as responsible. You may even sleep better at night. Besides feeling good by doing good, you're also getting a financial return. Although some investors are willing to surrender a proportion of their returns to contribute to a more sustainable world, responsible investing doesn't automatically lead to lower returns. You don't need to forgo performance at the expense of your values or conscience if you do your homework and carefully select the investments. Over the long run, price and value should converge.

Another benefit of sustainable investing is that you can choose your impact. For example, you may be interested in having a broad impact by investing in stocks or funds that meet various ESG requirements. You can also have targeted sustainability investments that support innovation in renewable energy and lower carbon emissions. Thus, your investment decisions can contribute to a net-zero economy by doing away with fossil fuels and other sources of emissions wherever possible. Additionally, you may choose to invest in companies or funds that foster minority empowerment, promote gender diversity, and support green projects. Because there are many different sustainable investments, you can build a tailor-made portfolio to meet your investment goals and values.

A final benefit of sustainable investing is psychological. If you invest in something you care about, you may stay invested longer and avoid the perils of jumping in and out of the market. Thus, by moving your money into such investments, you're achieving a win-win.

On the negative side, finding investments that meet your values while earning a reasonable financial return can be difficult because you're trying to meet two sets of goals. The best investments may not fit your definition of what you consider socially responsible or sustainable. Thus, you may be excluding the most profitable investment opportunities. On the other hand, socially responsible or sustainable companies may not be the best investments because they may make decisions hurting their profit-making abilities. Also, no business entity is entirely "clean." Thus, your task may be like finding the cleanest shirt in a basket of dirty laundry. Finally, creating ESG change requires patience since doing so is a long-term process requiring more than capitalism to achieve.

During the past half-century, sustainable investing has moved into the mainstream as more investors recognize its potential for attractive financial performance coupled with other benefits. For many investors, investing is more than putting money somewhere and hoping to get more back in the future. They want to avoid investing in companies that do objectionable things like exploiting workers, customers, or the environment. If they do invest in such companies, they're profiting from investments that are inconsistent with their values. Some are even willing, if necessary, to sacrifice some returns to sleep better. Thus, sustainable investing isn't a fad because it's increasing assets under management and fund offerings. In the future, a wave of sustainable investors is likely to hold companies even more accountable for their actions and enact consequences if they fail to adapt.

The remainder of this book contains six chapters. In Chapter 1, the journey begins by examining the changing investment landscape. This chapter provides context and sets the foundation for the rest of the book. Chapter 2 explores corporate social responsibility and the evolving responsibilities and obligations of a business. Chapter 3 focuses on the roles of social and religious values in shaping sustainable investing. Chapter 4 discusses the multitude of investment options available to sustainable investors. Chapter 5 reviews the performance implications of sustainable investing. This research-oriented chapter investigates the intriguing question, "Can sustainable investors have their cake and eat it too?" Finally, Chapter 6 focuses on building a portfolio with a purpose. Thus, let's begin the journey into the fascinating topic of sustainable investing.

1

THE CHANGING INVESTMENT LANDSCAPE

THE PAST, PRESENT, AND FUTURE

But beware! The time for all this is not yet. For at least another hundred years we must pretend to ourselves and to every one that fair is foul and foul is fair; for foul is useful and fair is not. Avarice and usury and precaution must be our gods for a little longer still. For only they can lead us out of the tunnel of economic necessity into the daylight.
—John Maynard Keynes

In 1930, during the Great Depression, John Maynard Keynes pondered what economic life would be like a century later. He believed that society would eventually value good over useful. Keynes expected that the wealthy would find more meaning in giving and that most people would have the economic necessities to live a meaningful life. He envisioned rising standards of living and shrinking workdays. Nine decades later, is society getting closer to Keynes's vision or is it farther away?

On the one hand, many corporate officers and investors still believe the 1987 *Wall Street* movie motto "Greed is good." Moreover, income inequality continues to grow, with most of the world's wealth and investments concentrated in the hands of a few. On the other hand, the ethics involving businesses and investors has changed over time, with many leaders endeavoring to quicken that change. For these change agents, the time is no longer near—it's now.

How did this responsible investor mindset develop? More specifically, how has sustainable investing evolved? *Sustainable investing* refers to any investment approach integrating environmental, social, and governance (ESG) factors into selecting and managing investments. Its long and rich history is rooted in the idea that investors can generate financial and extra-financial returns. In other words, sustainable investing allows investors to leverage their investments to make money and initiate changes in a company, their community, and the world. This investment philosophy represents a dramatic change from traditional investment and corporate philosophies that maximize shareholder value. In sharp contrast, sustainable investing advocates contend an almost obvious counterpoint: ethical values are valuable too.

Sustainable investing has become popular with investors, especially among younger generations. Today, no other alternative investment strategy generates the same type of capital inflows as sustainable investing. For example, its assets under management (AUM) quadrupled from $639 billion in 1995 to $3.07 trillion in 2010. In terms of market share, nearly one out of every eight dollars under professional management in 2010 was a sustainable asset. A growth rate of over 400% in only 15 years seemed impressive at the time, especially considering that the growth rate increased through the 2008 recession. Yet, sustainable asset growth hadn't even hit a peak. Sustainable assets grew at an astonishing pace. For example, in 2020, sustainable investing accounted for 33% of the total U.S. AUM. Between 2018 and 2020, total U.S.-domiciled sustainably invested AUM, both institutional and retail, grew 42%, to $17.1 trillion, up from $12 trillion.

In comparison to sustainable AUM, total AUM didn't grow at nearly the same pace. In 2018, sustainable AUM represented over one-third of all global AUM and almost half of all AUM in Europe. It's quickly becoming one of the major investment themes of the 21st century. As sustainable investments increased in AUM, they also grew to encompass a wide range of approaches applied for various asset classes. These approaches have evolved from socially responsible investing (SRI), including early exclusion criteria, to impact investing. This chapter explains the evolution of sustainable investing by exploring the past, present, and future issues that have established it as one of the most dominant forces in changing the current investment landscape.

What are the earliest origins of socially responsible investing (SRI) and corporate social responsibility (CSR)?

The term *SRI* is relatively new. *CSR* is a term that developed parallel to SRI but meant something entirely different. CSR isn't an investment model like SRI but rather a business model that attempts to hold firms accountable to all stakeholders. In other words, CSR is a top-down approach that focuses on corporate actions, whereas SRI is a bottom-up approach that focuses primarily on investor power. Chapter 2 provides further discussion of CSR.

Nonetheless, SRI and CSR are related. They're not identical twins, but their origins stem from social responsibility, dating back to the foundation of many religious and cultural traditions. For example, some scholars trace the social responsibility concepts of SRI and CSR to the Code of Hammurabi (1772 BC) or to the Vedic age in ancient India (1500–1000 BC). Moreover, all Abrahamic religions, whether Judaism, Christianity, or Islam, and even other religions like Buddhism, contain ancient teachings on using money ethically, especially usury. *Usury* is the unethical or immoral

> "Money was intended to be used in exchange, but not to increase at interest. And this term interest, which means the birth of money from money, is applied to the breeding of money because the offspring resembles the parent. Wherefore of all modes of getting wealth this is the most unnatural."
> —Aristotle

lending of money at high interest rates. Several famous Greek and Roman philosophers and statesmen, including Plato, Aristotle, Cato, Cicero, and Seneca, also condemned usury. The modern equivalent of a usurer is a *loan shark*. Although unethical, loan sharking isn't always illegal, such as *predatory lending* with unreasonably high interest rates. Two modern examples are *payday lending* and *title loans*. The structure of a payday loan is like a cash advance on the borrower's next payday. The borrower usually provides a postdated check to the lender for a portion of the borrower's future paycheck. A title loan is like a payday loan in that both are short-term loans at typically high interest rates. However, a critical difference is that a title loan is secured, often with the borrower using a vehicle title as collateral.

As for current usury rules within the Abrahamic religions, the Jewish religion prohibits usury among fellow Jews. Many Christians denounce usury, with the Catholic Church even imposing a universal prohibition on usury in the 12th century. Of all the Abrahamic religions, Islam may have the most stringent rules because Islam prohibits charging interest. To finance a purchase with a Muslim business owner, that owner may set a higher price with 0% interest.

Usury is one of the first immoral business practices affecting SRI and CSR efforts. Yet, it wasn't the worst business practice to be addressed by these efforts. A far more heinous business practice was slavery. *Abolitionism* was the movement to end slavery in America. In 1758, the Quakers were among the first abolitionists and activists to prohibit participation in the slave trade. Slavery takes many forms and still exists on a global scale. However, the abolitionists' efforts did play a key role in ending the Atlantic slave trade and slavery in the United States.

> "Having, first, gained all you can, and secondly saved all you can, then give all you can."
>
> —John Wesley

During the 18th century, John Wesley, a founder of the Methodist Church, outlined several basic tenets of SRI and CSR in his sermon, "The

Use of Money." Wesley discouraged profiting from unethical business practices, including usury, gaming, distilling liquor, and even tanning, which polluted local water sources with dangerous toxins. Hence, SRI and CSR evolved with the same ideals and values throughout the 18th century. However, during the 19th century, SRI and CSR began to go separate ways.

Who were the first drivers of SRI and CSR, and how did their efforts help establish the ways social responsibility activists affect corporate behavior?

Buddhism and Confucianism have partially inspired various corporate philanthropy elements, including *Shonindo*, which was developed around the beginning of the 18th century by a former Japanese merchant, Baigan Ishida (1685–1744). Shonindo, meaning "the way of the merchant," established principles for Japanese merchants as a counter to the samurai's more socially dominant ideology of the time, Bushido, meaning "the way of the warrior." Another socially responsible concept, pension plans, can be traced back to Great Britain, which developed a pension program for merchant seamen in the 1740s, expanded it to railroad workers in the 1840s, and eventually widened the program to cover other manual laborers. However, pension plans, like most employee benefits, were rare even well into the 19th century.

The Industrial Revolution began in Britain around 1750 and spread globally to Europe, the United States, and Japan. As mentioned earlier, many instances of social responsibility are part of a culture. However, the Industrial Revolution is a good starting point for tracing the genesis of modern CSR and SRI efforts because it created a new way of doing business and paved the way for banking and investing. Although many positive societal advances occurred during this time, several undesirable elements persisted. These included unhealthy living conditions, child labor, low wages, excessive working hours, six-day workweeks, few (if any) paid holidays or vacations, poor working conditions, often dangerous and toxic working environments, and environmental pollution. Within this context, several corporate philanthropists started to change the concepts of business and investing.

In 1810, a business owner named Robert Owen became one of the world's first social reformers in the United Kingdom. Owen tried several social experiments at his New Lanark Mill in Lanarkshire, including reducing the working day from 13 hours to 12 hours and eventually to 10 hours. Some credit Owen as the first person to call for an eight-hour workday by advocating that workers should have "eight hours labor, eight hours recreation, and eight hours rest." He greatly improved children's living and working conditions in New Lanark by only hiring children who were at least 10 years old. He also opened the first infant school in Great Britain at his mill to provide daycare for his employees' children. Additionally, Owen provided his employees with better-than-average wages, working conditions, training, and living conditions. He even covered his employees' wages for four months during an embargo against the United States during the War of 1812.

Owen also touted the increased profitability of his social efforts, but some of his partners didn't approve of the extra expenses. Frustrated with his partners, Owen created an early SRI example when he established a new firm in 1813 that further embraced his socially responsible views. His new partners agreed to accept his ethical and philanthropic goals if he provided a 5% return on their capital. William Allen, a well-known Quaker and abolitionist, and Jeremy Bentham, the founder of modern utilitarianism, were two notable stockholders in the new firm. From a business perspective, utilitarianism mirrors social responsibility in that it supports actions that maximize happiness and

> "The said truth is that it is the greatest happiness of the greatest number that is the measure of right and wrong."
>
> —Jeremy Bentham

well-being for all stakeholders instead of maximizing shareholder wealth.

Other early social responsibility trailblazers include the famous British chocolatiers George and Richard Cadbury. In 1893, the Cadburys began building employee housing, which they sold at cost. In 1893, John Henry Patterson, founder of the National Cash Register Company in Dayton, Ohio, constructed the first "daylight factory" buildings with floor-to-ceiling glass windows that improved lighting and provided ventilation for fresh air for his employees. Patterson also began providing them with other welfare benefits such as a dining room with low-cost hot lunches, exercise programs, baths, showers, a library, a clubhouse, a kindergarten for workers' children, social and professional clubs, and even an onsite doctor. The Cadburys visited the United States in 1901. They noted Patterson's management conditions, which marked a shift from their previous focus on housing conditions to a new emphasis on working conditions.

One of the most famous corporate philanthropists around this time was Andrew Carnegie, who would inspire many future business leaders with his writings, most notably *The Gospel of Wealth* in

> "Wealth is not to feed our egos but to feed the hungry and to help people help themselves."
>
> —Andrew Carnegie

1889. This work outlines the wealthy's social responsibility, including using their wealth to improve society for the greater good. Some other early corporate social reformers include Alfred Krupp (Germany), William Hesketh Lever and Charles Babbage (the United Kingdom), Nowrojee Wadia, Jamsetji Tata, and Mahatma Gandhi (India), and John D. Rockefeller (the United States). Most of these individuals focused on either income inequality or social responsibility, but a few, like Babbage, emphasized pollution issues. Despite the engagement of many visionaries in modern social and environmental reforms during the 18th and 19th centuries, such reforms didn't spread rapidly. For much of the 19th century, business

owners and workers, albeit less enthusiastically, generally preferred a laissez-faire approach or even Herbert Spencer's ideas
on *social Darwinism*. More specifically, they believed that biological concepts such as natural selection and survival of the
fittest were the better constructs for developing a business philosophy. Ironically, as the workforce evolved into the 20th century, social responsibility concepts grew stronger while public
acceptance of social Darwinism faded.

What is screening, and why is it important?

Although early examples of SRI and CSR often focused on
CSR, SRI gained a foothold in the 20th century. Since SRI's
history may be more relevant from an investor's perspective,
screening for relevant SRI examples seems prudent. Many consider screening as the foundation of modern SRI. *Screening* is a
process of searching for investments that meet specific social,
environmental, and governance criteria. One of the first recorded examples of screening using social criteria occurred in
1928 when Philip Carret founded Fidelity Mutual Trust, which
later became the Pioneer Fund. Some credit the Pioneer Fund
as the first mutual fund to use social screening criteria.

Two types of screening are available: *negative screening* and
positive screening.

- *Negative screening.* Negative screening came first as the
  Pioneer Fund excluded certain types of stocks that sold
  alcohol and tobacco. The earliest screening was negative
  screening, as many companies wanted to filter out stocks
  that didn't agree with their values. Some of the early so-
  called sin stocks focused on companies involved with the
  alcohol, tobacco, gaming (i.e., gambling), weapons, and sex
  industries. Thus, negative screening uses exclusion criteria.
- *Positive screening.* By contrast, positive or affirmative
  screening was more of an inclusionary process and sought
  to add the stocks of companies that provided one or more

positive benefits for communities, the world, or various stakeholders.

In this way, screening's greatest attribute allows investors to vote for their beliefs and priorities. In short, investing could now offer both a financial and nonfinancial return.

What were the most critical milestones in the 20th century for SRI?

The modern precursors of the social responsibility movement that led to SRI consist of two periods.

- *The 1940s and 1950s.* Around the middle of the 20th century, various trade unions began focusing on achieving socially responsible goals with their pension fund assets. Three of the earliest examples were the United Mine Workers of America (UMWA), the International Brotherhood of Electrical Workers (IBEW), and the International Ladies' Garment Workers' Union (ILGWU). The former union established a multi-employer welfare and retirement fund that invested heavily in the Appalachia area's medical facilities. In contrast, the two latter unions created funds that sponsored various housing projects.

  "I knew that America would never invest the necessary funds of energies in rehabilitation of its poor as long as adventures like Vietnam continued to draw men and skills and money like some demonic destructive suction tube."
  —Martin Luther King Jr.

- *The 1960s and 1970s.* This period added additional momentum to many ongoing labor issues and created a new wave of accountability with the feminist, civil rights, and antiwar movements. These movements would add new SRI elements that addressed the issues of gender equality, social justice, and weapons manufacturing. These initiatives included the rise of economic development projects like those championed by Dr. Martin Luther King Jr., such as the Montgomery bus boycott and Operation Breadbasket Project in Chicago. Like many other social activists during this period, King also voiced his concerns about the Vietnam War to social investors. In response to these concerns, the early 1970s gave rise to the Pax World Fund, an antiwar SRI fund that avoided investing in weapon contractors such as Dow Chemical. Dow Chemical manufactured the infamous chemical weapons Agent Orange and napalm. The pictures of napalm burning Vietnamese children's backs left an indelible impression on Americans' minds, turning many people against the war.

How did these earlier milestones in the 20th century help establish how SRI activists could affect corporate behavior?

These earlier periods paved the way to a third period, the 1980s and 1990s, which showed SRI's global reach. SRI's most influential example is probably the boycott of South Africa's apartheid regime. Apartheid was a system created in 1948 by the Afrikaner National Party that allowed the white minority to rule the black majority through state-sanctioned racial segregation. Although apartheid intended to ease the concerns of the wealthier whites in South Africa, it essentially condemned most of the black population to poverty with almost no chance for upward mobility. Apartheid began to gain international opposition in 1960 following the state-sponsored Sharpeville massacre, during which the South African police killed 69 black protesters. The United Nations (UN)

"Starting with the work place, I tightened the screws step by step and raised the bar step by step. Eventually I got to the point where I said that companies must practice corporate civil disobedience against the laws and I threatened South Africa and said in two years Mandela must be freed, apartheid must end, and blacks must vote or else I'll bring every American company I can out of South Africa."

—Reverend Leon Sullivan

imposed a voluntary arms embargo against South Africa in 1963. The boycott became mandatory in 1976 after yet another deadly protest, the Soweto Uprising. This event began with about 20,000 Sowetan students protesting the strict language requirements for their schools. However, the uprising ended with around 700 student deaths and 4,000 student injuries.

After the Soweto Uprising, Reverend Leon Sullivan, a board member of General Motors, created the Sullivan Principles, which outlined a code of conduct for practicing business in South Africa. After disclosure that many U.S. companies were not following the spirit of the Sullivan Principles, numerous colleges, universities, faith-based groups, and pension funds began to protest in a new way. These groups collectively began divesting from companies doing business in South Africa. In what will likely remain the most crucial moment of SRI's influential history, these divestments continued throughout the 1980s, including a mandatory ban in 1986 on new South African investments by American and European governments. The ensuing lack of capital flowing into the country forced nearly 75% of South Africa's employers to draft legislation to end apartheid. South Africans officially dissolved apartheid in 1994 by voting the apartheid regime out of power. In hindsight, some academic debate exists about shareholder boycotts' impact on the financial markets. Some research indicates that South African divestment had a more substantial perceived impact than an empirical one. Nonetheless, SRI efforts played a highly public role in protesting apartheid. Therefore, SRI received much credit for bringing this period in history to a close.

Who created the first modern SRI index?

Although many investment funds began to employ SRI principles and strategies in the 20th century, SRI indices didn't appear until the 1990s. An SRI index's unbiased methodology offers several advantages over a typical SRI fund, including increased transparency, lower transaction costs, fewer market timing issues, and hardly any of the additional fees and biases that come with using a fund manager. The social research firm Kinder, Lydenberg, Domini & Co. (KLD) constructed one of the earliest and most successful SRI indices, the Domini Social 400 Index (DSI), which has evolved to become the MSCI KLD 400 Social Index. Like other SRI funds of the time, the DSI initially relied heavily on negative screening and excluded companies involved with alcohol, tobacco, gaming, weapons manufacturing, and nuclear power. However, KLD was also one of the first firms to embrace positive screening fully. It created a ranking system for product quality, corporate citizenship, and equality standards for women and minorities.

How did environmental, social, and governance (ESG) criteria become the three primary social responsibility factors?

Several investment firms quickly followed in KLD's footsteps. They began tracking SRI data and creating SRI funds and indices. However, no agreed-upon methodology existed for tracking SRI data. Eventually, almost all screening criteria, including both positive and negative screening criteria, would be categorized into three main categories: environmental, social, and governance.

ESG has a somewhat romantic beginning. The idea was conceived in 2004 when former UN Secretary General Kofi Annan invited 50 chief executive officers (CEOs) from the world's largest financial institutions to participate in a joint effort to integrate ESG into capital markets. ESG was officially born in 2005 during the "Who Cares Wins" conference in Zurich in what would become a watershed moment for SRI. These three factors would represent three rivers emptied into one joint SRI basin like a naturally occurring watershed. However, as rivers do over time, these three value-drivers also began to change the SRI landscape.

Before ESG investing, religious values and moral criteria, which predominantly used negative screening to avoid the previously mentioned sin stocks, were SRI's primary basis. Early ESG proponents argued that ESG criteria were better because they had social and financial relevance. Moreover, many of the world's largest financial institutions agreed and publicly endorsed ESG principles. They collectively reasoned that as the world becomes more globalized and interconnected, corporations that focus on improving specific ESG issues can increase shareholder value by including better risk management, preparedness for regulatory action, and insights into new markets. Also, ESG proponents believe that focusing on ESG criteria has developed more sustainable markets, stronger communities, and a better world. Figure 1.1 shows a few examples of specific ESG principles.

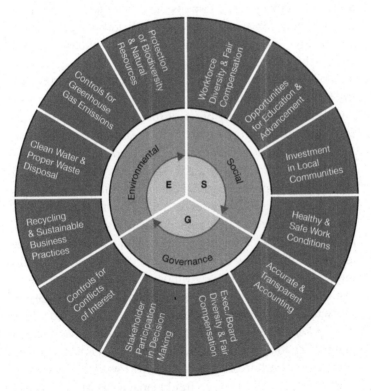

Figure 1.1 Examples of ESG Principles

What are other vital issues in the 21st century for SRI and CSR besides ESG criteria?

A critical issue for ESG proponents concerns how to create actionable and measurable goals to hold corporations accountable. Like the formation of ESG criteria, the UN once again played an essential role in creating the Sustainable Development Goals (SDGs). In 2015, the UN General Assembly outlined 17 SDGs to ensure a sustainable future for all humankind. The SDGs are: (1) no poverty, (2) zero hunger, (3) good health and well-being, (4) quality education, (5) gender equality, (6) clean water and sanitation, (7) affordable and clean energy, (8) decent work and economic growth, (9) industry, innovation, and infrastructure, (10) reducing inequality, (11) sustainable cities and communities, (12) responsible consumption and production, (13) climate action, (14) life below water, (15) life on land, (16) peace, justice, and strong institutions, and (17) partnerships for the goals.

Global implementation of the SDGs began in 2016. In 2017, the UN created specific targets for each goal and added various tools for monitoring progress toward the goals. Although some goals didn't receive end dates, most had a target date between 2020 and 2030. In 2018, the UN launched SDG-Tracker online to track progress toward these SDGs. It's based at Oxford University and provides global data across all indicators.

Achieving the SDGs is expensive. Reaching all the SDG goals could cost roughly $4 trillion, according to UN estimates. In 2018, the Basel Institute of Commons and Economics estimated that annual costs for achieving all SDGs would range between $2.5 and $5.0 trillion. Although the UN would like everyone to play a role in achieving these goals, SRI is likely to play a critical role in fulfilling the SDG agenda. Like the Rockefeller Foundation, many foundations have stated that the key to financing and achieving the SDGs is mobilizing a substantial portion of investment flows toward development efforts. Surprisingly, pension fund managers agree. The World Pensions Council (WPC) now holds ESG-focused discussions as part of its annual plan, and pension fund trustees have started to shift the whole investment system toward SDG-driven investment.

What are the main ways that investors can participate in SRI and SDG efforts?

Three primary tools are available for participating in SRI and SDG efforts. The first and most common tool is screening investments based on specific values and goals, such as ESG criteria. Although this tool doesn't always create immediate change, it can produce long-term change in corporate culture, such as the divestment in South Africa during apartheid, generating rippling effects. For example, after seeing how helpful a tool divestment was against apartheid, the Sudanese government created the Sudan Divestment Task Force in 2006 to address the ongoing genocide and suffering in Sudan's war-battered region of Darfur. The United States led the way and enacted the Sudan Accountability and Divestment Act of 2007, which pressured the Sudanese government to end the civil war and helped South Sudan gain its independence in 2011.

> "Each time a man stands up for an ideal, or acts to improve the lot of others, or strikes out against injustice, he sends forth a tiny ripple of hope, and crossing each other from a million different centers of energy and daring those ripples build a current which can sweep down the mightiest walls of oppression and resistance."
> —Robert F. Kennedy

The second tool is shareholder activism. It provides a more direct route to corporate change by giving shareholders the right to participate in corporate governance through proxy voting actively. One of the most significant proxy issues is board composition, which facilitates the ability of shareholders to vote out board members who don't support shareholder values. For instance, the New York City Pension Fund publicly launched the Boardroom Accountability Project in 2014.

This project gave long-term shareholders the right to nominate and place a limited number of alternative board directors at U.S. companies via a corporate ballot or proxy card. This "proxy access" provided pensioners with a meaningful way to hold boards accountable and obtain board diversity information, including the directors' race, gender, and qualifications.

The third and final tool is community development. It allows investors to connect directly with those in need. Several examples include community development loans, community development banks, and community development credit unions. A critical difference between the latter two is that banks are for-profit while credit unions are nonprofit institutions. Regardless, all these community programs can become an alternative source of cash for reviving distressed communities. Investors can invest directly in their community in many other ways.

This chapter identifies some emerging trends stemming from SRI, including sustainable investing, green investing, impact investing, and community investing. All these investment strategies have a strong connection to community development.

What are the similarities and differences between sustainable investing and green investing?

Sustainable investing can involve several different strategies. Those discussed in this chapter are green investing, impact investing, and community investing. All are related, but some are more similar than others. Before comparing sustainable investing with green investing, some people use sustainable investing interchangeably with responsible investing. Others contend that responsible investments focus more on the current impact.

In contrast, sustainable investments emphasize the long-term effects or the sustainability of the short-term impact. Thus, sustainable companies employ sustainability practices like increased board accountability, proper hiring standards, stronger relations with external stakeholders, transparency and consistency in reporting processes, and various environmental practices. Environmental practices may include using recycled materials, reducing waste, adopting clean and renewable energy, reducing carbon footprints, and preventing or controlling pollution. Other such practices are conserving and protecting water sources, engaging in free-range and organic farming, securing sustainable fisheries, constructing green builds with environmentally responsible techniques, and greening the planet through planting trees.

As for sustainable investing versus green investing, both seek sustainable investment strategies without causing harm to the environment. The real difference is that sustainable investing encompasses all three ESG criteria, whereas green investing focuses primarily on environmental issues, the E in ESG. Adding in profit as a consideration enables further differentiation between sustainable and green investing. Sustainable investing considers the *triple bottom line* (TBL). According to TBL proponents, companies should focus on social and environmental concerns as they do on profits. John Elkington, the sustainability guru, coined TBL in 1994 and advocates maximizing profits and the benefits for people and the planet. Thus, sustainability investors add the third return—the environmental return—to accompany financial and social returns.

Compared to sustainable investing, green investing isn't as balanced and tends to emphasize the environmental return. The green investors' primary concern is maximizing the planet's benefits by conserving natural resources and promoting environmentally friendly business practices. Thus,

> "To truly shift the needle, however, we need a new wave of TBL innovation and deployment . . . working toward a triple helix for value creation, a genetic code for tomorrow's capitalism, spurring the regeneration of our economies, societies, and biosphere."
> —John Elkington

> "Listen up, you couch potatoes: each recycled beer can save enough electricity to run a television for three hours."
>
> —Dennis Hayes

green investing is a subset of sustainable investing and includes the same environmental practices previously mentioned.

Two early crusaders for sustainable and green investing were Dennis Hayes and Joan Bavaria. Hayes coordinated the first Earth Day in 1970 and expanded the Earth Day Network to more than 180 nations. In 1999, *Time Magazine* named him the "Hero of the Planet." Bavaria founded both the Social Investment Forum (1981) and Trillium (1982). The Social Investment Forum (now known as US SIF or The Forum for Sustainable and Responsible Investment) is a U.S. association that provides research and support to advance sustainable investing across all asset classes. Trillium Asset Management claims to be the "oldest investment advisor exclusively focused on sustainable and responsible investing."

At the helm of Trillium, Bavaria helped pioneer numerous organizations in the sustainable investing field. For example, in 1989, she allied with leading environmentalists like Hayes to create the Coalition for Environmentally Responsible EconomieS (CERES). CERES, later rebranded as Ceres, is a network for green investors, environmental organizations, and other public interest groups to address environmental concerns. Ceres created the Valdez Principles, now known as the Ceres Principles, which set forth a 10-point environmental code of conduct following the *Exxon Valdez* spill in 1989. The Exxon Valdez, an oil supertanker owned by Exxon Shipping Company, struck a reef on its way to Long Beach, California. Many companies have publicly endorsed the Ceres Principles since their inception, and Ceres continues to be highly influential in the sustainable investing space. For instance, Ceres and the UN sponsored an annual Investor Summit on Climate Risk in 2016. Over 110 institutional investors agreed on the goal of doubling global investment in clean energy by 2020.

What are the similarities and differences between impact investing and community investing?

Impact and community investors generally invest more locally than other sustainable investors. Usually, impact investing involves providing capital to address social and envi-

"Money must serve, not rule."
—Pope Francis

ronmental issues. It can even include investing in nonprofits. One defining attribute of impact investing is that it focuses on positive screening, not negative screening activities. Religious organizations have a long history of participating in faith-based impact investing activities. The Catholic Church even has its own Vatican Conference on Impact Investing. Some contend that impact investing places emphasis on the social return rather than on a financial return. Although many impact investors still want a financial return, they usually view a measurable and beneficial social or environmental impact as critical. Impact investing occurs in developed and emerging markets. *Emerging markets*, also known as *emerging economies* or *developing countries*, are nations that invest in more productive capacity. Impact investing can involve various asset classes like private equity, venture capital, and debt. Recent examples include investments in clean technology, community development, and microfinance. *Microfinance* provides financial services to small businesses and low-income or unemployed people who don't qualify for conventional banking and related services.

Like impact investing, community investing includes public and private investment to low-income and other underserved communities. The only real difference between impact investing and community investing is that impact investing focuses on a specific cause, whereas community investing emphasizes a particular community. Community investment also means investing directly in an institution through cash or low-interest debt instead of buying stock. Common examples include community development banks, community development corporátions, credit unions, microfinance institutions, and small business investment companies. Thus, investors often use impact investing and community investing interchangeably. Both strategies focus on investments at a more local level, and these investments could include money and time spent on mentoring people or advising start-up companies.

Figure 1.2 provides a matrix that categorizes community investing, impact investing, green investing, and traditional SRI screening and ESG investing under the sustainable investing umbrella. Due to the generic and often interchangeable use of these terms, they don't necessarily fit as neatly in one quadrant or circle, as shown later in this chapter. However, the matrix does provide a possible framework for evolving each quadrant and showing how sustainable investing has grown to encompass a broader range of ideas and applications.

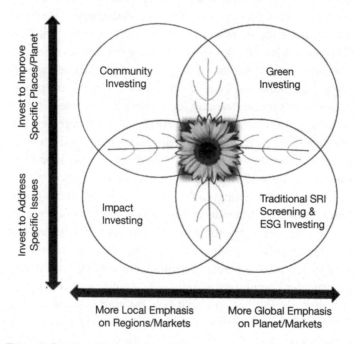

Figure 1.2 Sustainable Investing Matrix

How have risk tolerances and investment preferences changed from a generational perspective?

Each country has its own cultural and political experiences and milestones that often don't match each other. One country may experience peaceful and robust economic times while another has a civil war. Thus, the characterization of each generation often differs. Here is how the United States categorizes the generations.

- The greatest generation or "GI generation" (born 1901–1927) came of age during the Roaring Twenties, lived through the Great Depression, and included veterans who fought in World War II (WWII).
- The silent generation or the "lucky few" (born 1928–1945) came of age after WWII and included many Korean War and Vietnam War veterans.
- Baby boomers, or the "me generation" (born 1946–1964), were born after WWII. Although many older baby boomers were veterans or supporters of the Vietnam War, a large percentage of the younger baby boomers participated in the rise of the counterculture of the 1960s. Many social justice and antiwar movements started at this time. As a result, the following generations include a shrinking percentage of veterans and an increasing number of females and minorities in the workplace.

  > "World War II brought the Greatest Generation together. Vietnam tore the Baby Boomers apart."
  > —Jim Webb

- Younger generations include Generation X or "Gen X" (born 1965–1980), Generation Y or "millennials" (born 1981–1996), Generation Z or "Gen Z" or zoomers (born 1997–2012), and the new Generation Alpha or "Gen Alpha" (born after 2012).

Figure 1.3 places these generations on a timeline, with several important dates illustrating the rapid rise of sustainable

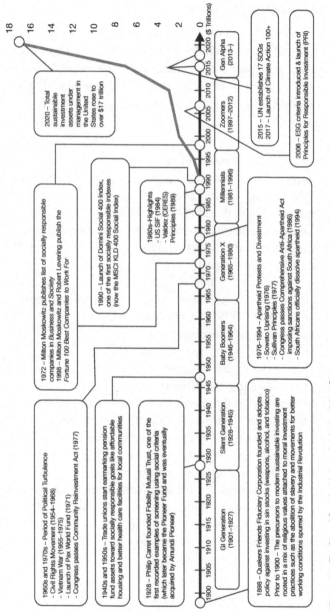

Figure 1.3 The Rise of Sustainable Investing in the United States

investing. Notice the growth in AUM over the last three decades. This trend will likely continue, considering that newer generations are growing up with sustainable investing and are far more likely to prefer sustainable investments.

During the natural transfer of wealth between generations, monumental market impacts can occur when the generations hold fundamentally different beliefs. In the United States, trillions of dollars in wealth are moving from the silent generation and baby boomers to Gen X and millennials. This wealth transfer is likely to increase faster throughout the 2020s as the baby boomers' numbers decrease. As of 2019, the total number of millennials (72.1 million) has officially surpassed baby boomers (69.6 million). Gen Z (67.2 million) and Gen X (65.2 million) were third and fourth. Only a small number of the silent generation (20.9 million) and the GI generation (1.7 million) are still alive. Many investment firms currently pay close attention to baby boomers and millennials because they had much higher birth rates than the other generations. A stark contrast exists in their values and priorities.

Baby boomers and millennials have several distinguishing characteristics. For instance, a higher percentage of baby boomers prefer using a "buy-and-hold" investment strategy than millennials. The rationale is that baby boomers are more likely to trust financial markets, are far more interested in investing for retirement than millennials, and are more concerned with passing on an inheritance. On the other hand, millennials show greater interest in investing for shorter-term goals like saving for a vacation, a home upgrade, or a home purchase. Additionally, they're more interested in saving money by cohabitating with family and friends, using car-sharing services, or delaying marriage. Millennials view marriage as more a financial commitment than a romantic one. They often wait an additional five or more years to make sure they're financially stable and can afford expenses like engagement rings, weddings, honeymoons, and a down payment on a house.

Millennials tend to delay many life decisions, purchases, and investment plans compared to prior generations. This trend makes sense considering they lived through several difficult economic downturns, stayed in school longer, spent more on rising college expenses, and incurred more student loan debt. Millennials have also accepted more temporary jobs and faced more stagnant incomes than previous generations while balancing rising housing and health care costs. As a result, they watch their expenses more closely and have developed a different mindset and relationship with money than baby boomers. For instance, millennials are far more likely to use technology like *robo-advisors*. These advisors are automated investing platforms and services that use algorithms to create desired asset allocations at far cheaper rates than traditional financial advisors.

Millennials also have higher risk aversion and lower trust in the financial markets. This characteristic shouldn't be surprising given that their formative years included the dot-com bubble burst of the early 2000s, the devastating housing and financial crisis in 2008, and the economic shutdown in 2020 due to the COVID-19 pandemic. These experiences have led millennials to be more likely to hoard cash, purchase real estate, and buy precious metals and cryptocurrencies. They're also more interested in investing in themselves through either education or starting their own business. Millennials prefer allocating more of their resources to experiences over material goods. Finally, they place a greater value on living their lives in more sustainable ways and are twice as likely to support sustainable investing than baby boomers. In short, millennials see sustainable investing as a way to reward good companies and punish bad companies for how they treat all stakeholders.

What impact are millennials and progressive politics making on sustainable investing?

Millennials are the largest, most diverse, and most progressive generation in U.S. history. Diversity plays a key role in millennials' progressive philosophy because women and minorities are far more likely to identify as progressive. Each year, the Democratic advantage among millennial voters grows. Even millennials who identify as Republicans generally have more progressive views than older political party members, especially with climate change concerns and social issues like immigration, gender equality, and marriage equality. For example, millennials are far more likely to protest economic inequality, large corporation and financial institutions' greed, and corruption than baby boomers. Many Gen Xers and millennials are far more likely than baby boomers to participate in or support the 21st century's major movements, such as the 2011 Occupy Wall Street movement and the similar Blockupy movement in Europe. They also are more likely to participate in social movements that address human rights abuses and corruption. Examples include the Black Lives Matter movement in the United States, the Los Indignados movement in Spain, the People Power Movement in Uganda, and the Free Hong Kong movement against China. Another U.S. example is the Fight for $15. This movement started in 2012 and advocates raising the minimum wage to $15 per hour.

From an environmental standpoint, the younger generations are leading the way for action on climate change. For instance, they're far more likely to support the Green New Deal, first coined by Thomas Friedman in 2007 and referring to the New Deal enacted by President Franklin D. Roosevelt in the 1930s. The Green New Deal is a legislative platform sponsored by Congress's progressive members and proposes legislative reforms to address climate change and economic inequality. Gen X and

> "If you put a windmill in your yard or some solar panels on your roof, bless your heart. But we will only green the world when we change the very nature of the electricity grid . . . like the New Deal, if we undertake the green version, it has the potential to create a whole new clean power industry to spur our economy into the 21st century."
>
> —Thomas Friedman

Millennials are also more likely to protest specific environmental concerns. For example, they're more active in protesting pipeline construction. Examples include the Dakota Access Pipeline from North Dakota to Illinois, the Permian Highway Pipeline from West Texas to the Gulf Coast, the Atlantic Coast Pipeline from West Virginia to North Carolina, and the Keystone XL Pipeline from Western Canada to Nebraska.

What are the conservative politics of sustainable investing in terms of advocacy agenda?

> "I studied what principles under-laid peace and prosperity and concluded that the only way to achieve societal well-being was through a system of economic freedom."
>
> —Charles Koch

From a conservative standpoint, winning back the youth is the focus of various foundations and groups. These groups have substantial financial backing from conservative business leaders, most notably David and Charles Koch of Koch Industries, the largest U.S. privately held company. Two conservative movements that gained traction in the United States in the 21st century are the Tea Party movement, which began in 2009, and the Make America Great Again (MAGA) movement, which helped elect Donald Trump U.S. president in 2016. The Tea Party movement is a take on the Boston Tea Party, a protest in 1773 by the Sons of Liberty in Boston, Massachusetts, against the British Parliament's tax on tea. The protesters destroyed an entire shipment of British tea to declare "no taxation without representation." On this historical premise, members of the Tea Party movement in the 21st century called for lower taxes, decreased government spending, and reduced national debt.

Concerning the MAGA movement, the phrase has a long history with presidential campaigns, going back to 1940 and 1964. In more recent times, Ronald Reagan also said, "Let's Make America Great Again" during his 1980 presidential campaign. Bill Clinton used the phrase again during his victorious

1992 presidential campaign, and Hillary Clinton used it in her unsuccessful 2008 presidential campaign. Regardless, the MAGA movement is most associated with Donald Trump, furthering the divide between conservative and progressive viewpoints.

On the right side of the political spectrum, many conservatives believed the United States was declining. They were apprehensive about the rise of Democratic socialism. On the left side, many progressives thought the United States was never that great and viewed the MAGA movement as nothing more than a racist attempt to "Make America White Again." Other progressives offered slogans, including "Make Earth Greta Again," referring to the young Swedish environmental activist Greta Thunberg. In short, although these conservative movements gained some support from millennials, progressive movements are still gaining support from millennials at a far faster pace.

What is the divide between progressive and conservative investors?

Although many progressive funds align more closely with traditional sustainable funds and SDGs, conservatives have created investment strategies and products. Most conservatives are more likely to buy from and invest in pro-conservative companies. These companies tend to make their products in the United States and support the U.S. Constitution's First and Second Amendments. The First Amendment provides freedom of speech, which is vital to conservatives regarding religious expression. The Second Amendment protects the right to keep and bear arms. For example, conservatives are more likely to invest in precious metals, guns, and ammunition. They tend to support companies that manufacture weapons like Remington, "America's Oldest Gunmaker." Additionally, they're inclined to invest in companies supporting the military, like the Black Rifle Coffee Company, which pledged in

2017 to hire 10,000 veterans after Starbucks pledged to hire 10,000 refugees.

Several conservative websites and media outlets inform conservative investors about companies they should support and boycott. For example, some well-known Christian-based companies like Chick-fil-A and Hobby Lobby are private, meaning investors can only support them through purchases. Nonetheless, Hobby Lobby still maintains strong support from conservative groups. Yet, conservatives downgraded Chick-fil-A after it ended its donations to conservative Christian organizations in 2019 and donated to more progressive organizations like the Southern Poverty Law Center. Conservatives tend to support companies that fiscally and openly support conservative causes. More current examples include oil companies like ExxonMobil, retailers of outdoor recreation merchandise like Bass Pro Shops, and companies that openly support Christian values like Tyson Foods.

Moreover, researchers report that many fund managers invest more in companies led by executives who share their political ideologies or party affiliations. Thus, it's not surprising that one outcome of the growing political divide, especially between baby boomers and millennials, is the emergence of politically themed investment funds. For instance, the Point Bridge Capital MAGA ETF, with the easy-to-remember ticker MAGA, allows conservative investors to invest in companies that support their Republican ideology. Although targeted investment funds may seem strange, investment funds are now available for all kinds of investors with vastly different value systems. There are even investment funds for investors that prefer sin stocks like the Vice Fund, which is now the USA Mutuals Vitium Global Fund (VICEX). VICEX invests at least 80% of its AUM into sin stock industries like alcoholic beverages, tobacco, gaming, and defense/aerospace.

As for Democrats, endless investment products are available. As previously stated, most ESG criteria, SDGs, and current sustainable products align more closely with progressive ideals. For instance, Calvert Investments created the Calvert Social Index. It also offers various progressive index funds. Most ETFs based on sustainable indices are considered progressive, including iShares MSCI KLD 400 Social ETF (DSI), iShares MSCI ACWI Low Carbon Target ETF (CRBN), TIAA-CREF's Social Choice Equity Fund (TICRX), and State Street's Gender Diversity Index (given the appropriate ticker SHE). Pax Ellevate Global Women's Leadership Fund (PXWIX) is a mutual fund focusing on gender diversity. Investors should also check to see if the net expense ratio is higher. Although the expense ratio for PXWIX is only 0.56%, other mutual funds for progressives are more expensive. For example, Trillium's Portfolio 21 Global Equity Fund Class R (PORTX) is a highly regarded mutual fund, but its net expense ratio is relatively high at around 1.33%. Progressives who want to invest in specific companies also have many options, including most large tech stocks like FAANG stocks (Meta, formerly Facebook, Apple, Amazon, Netflix, and Google). Other companies rated highly by progressives and liberals are Johnson & Johnson, Intel, Costco Wholesale, Nvidia, Adobe, IBM, Salesforce, PayPal, Cisco, CVS Health, Microsoft, IKEA, ZipCar, Tesla, SodaStream, Beyond Meat, First Solar, Starbucks, and Disney.

What trends are likely to drive the future of the sustainable investing industry?

Perhaps the most controversial trend is the role of governments in the sustainable investing space. Although politics has many nuances, one central issue in politics has always been how to balance the progressive efforts toward social justice with conservative efforts to maintain individual liberty. For example, a growing interest exists in increasing taxes on corporations, capital gains, dividends, and trading to finance various social reforms.

> "The political problem of mankind is to combine three things: economic efficiency, social justice, and individual liberty."
> —John Maynard Keynes

Governments also seem increasingly engaged in making more significant investments into the sustainable investing space, including direct investments, subsidies, and tax breaks for "green" industries. Moreover, while governments provide specific industries with "carrots," they hit others with "sticks" via increased regulation. For instance, many coal and oil companies may soon face unsurmountable rules that may cripple their ability to compete with more renewable energy industries. In short, the future impact of governments on specific industries can be dramatic. If governments issue enough carrots and sticks, the value of green stocks may soon race past other stocks in the same way that tech stocks have outpaced the market since the 1990s.

> "I'm worried about green washing. I think we should come down on it very, very hard, whether it's with criminal intent or actively deceptive."
>
> —John Elkington

With or without government help, green investing is likely here to stay. However, one negative trend is *greenwashing*, which is false green marketing designed to deceive or mislead the public into believing that a company's products, goals, and policies are environmentally friendly. Greenwashing isn't a new concept. The environmentalist Jay Westervelt coined the word in 1986 to describe the hotel practice of placing placards in each room, encouraging guests to save the planet by reusing towels. He argued that the real goal of these hotels was to increase profits. Companies can engage in greenwashing by making misleading, unsubstantiated, vague, erroneous, irrelevant, insignificant, and false claims. Some of the worst offenders are *green scammers*, who create environmentally friendly sounding names for products and organizations to provide information and research that misinforms the public and investors.

A clear example is the denial of human-made global warming by green scamming organizations founded by big oil companies like ExxonMobil. In a tactic similar to greenwashing, many companies and organizations falsely promote or mislead the public about their social and corporate governance policies. In general, the most significant negative trend for sustainable investing is likely to be misinformation cloaked in the form of ESG window dressing. In other words, how many future firms and investment products will be wolves masquerading in sheep's clothing?

Even when sustainable investors have honest ESG data, they may have difficulty interpreting them. Many companies and investment firms believe they have a fiduciary duty to employ some ESG practices for various reasons, including proper risk management. Most investment funds may soon truthfully claim that they incorporate sustainable elements in some form or fashion. Thus, the biggest challenge for sustainable investors is the absence of a consistent methodology and standardized regulations for measuring and analyzing ESG data. Creating ESG data and SDGs has helped, but several questions remain. For example, which companies have a higher ranking—those always having high ESG scores or companies improving their ESG scores? Without precise, objective, and comparable data, sustainable investors may shift their focus to financial data.

Several positive future trends may emerge for sustainable investing. For example, various parties are refining ESG data collection methods that may mitigate data issues like transparency. Additionally, market participants are creating nuanced products for specific interest groups. For example, *gender lens investing* strategies have recently surfaced to promote gender equality in the workplace.

However, the most promising positive trend may be sustainable investing's growing ability to finance critical societal goals like SDGs. SDGs may quickly evolve too. Consider the COVID-19 pandemic. Several notable sustainable investors like Bill Gates and Dolly Parton have invested heavily in medical companies to create a safe vaccine for the coronavirus. What other promising future research in health care will sustainable investors support? Can sustainable investing become a crucial weapon in combatting changing disease patterns and promoting healthy lifestyles? The answer is most likely yes. The California State Teachers' Retirement System (CalSTRS) recently divested more than $237 million in tobacco holdings from its investment portfolio. What's next? Can sustainable investors help fund solutions for climate change issues like population growth, the rising water table, and the subsequent migration of millions of people? Will sustainable investing help fund space exploration or focus more on protecting Earth's natural resources? Will sustainable investors support future technology growth or combat it? What about the rise of artificial intelligence (AI), cyborgs, genetically designed humans, and robots? Will sustainable investors fight them as terrorists or help protect their rights in the future? Will a quadruple bottom line emerge? In short, sustainable investing's future is likely to represent humanity's list of priorities. The idea of investors voting with their wallets or purses has never rung truer. For many investors, the time for waiting for change has passed. Sustainable investors have declared that the future is now.

Takeaways

"A society grows great when old men plant trees whose shade they know they shall never sit in."
—Greek Proverb

Today, sustainable investing's momentum continues to grow. More investors than ever want their investments to create a financial return and an extra-financial return. Each new generation appears more progressive and serious about sustainable investing than the last. Sustainable investing has the potential to play an important role in addressing and solving many of society's most significant problems.

The evolution of sustainable investing from a fringe idea to one of the most dominant investment strategies of the 20th century may force academics and others to revisit many long-held traditional investment theories. Yet, reshaping the investment landscape requires more time. The one forecast that seems safe to predict is that sustainable investing is here to stay for the foreseeable future. Here are some key takeaways from this chapter:

- Recognize that sustainable investing has grown from its original religious, cultural, and SRI focus to include different approaches.
- Be aware that sustainable investing has its historical roots in negative screening and initially focused on avoiding "sin" stocks.
- Consider other ways besides screening to participate in sustainable investing, such as proxy voting and direct investing at the community level.
- Match specific SDGs with their corresponding ESG criteria to identify sustainable investments that reflect your values.
- Consider how millennials and progressives affect financial markets.
- Be wary of greenwashing and other window-dressing techniques.
- Be patient as sustainable investing grows to meet investors' demands and as information and tracking methods improve.
- Check on growing trends like nuanced products for specific interest groups.
- Keep in mind that the most positive short-term sustainable investing trends are likely to be investing to address specific SDGs.
- Consider that the most favorable long-term sustainable investing trends are likely to address growing concerns in technology, health care, income inequality, and climate change.

2

CORPORATE SOCIAL RESPONSIBILITY

DELIVERING BOTH PROFIT AND PURPOSE

> Creating a strong business and building a better world are not conflicting goals—they are both essential ingredients for long-term success.
>
> —William Clay Ford Jr.

What are the responsibilities and obligations of a business? The answer has been evolving for decades. The original capitalist view of a corporation is that its primary goal is to create wealth for its owners. For public companies, the owners are the stockholders. This perspective focuses on generating profits to maximize a company's stock price. Any deviation from this goal is likely to increase costs and decrease both profits and stock value. However, over time, other perspectives became popular. For example, allocating resources toward employees' well-being may cost more, but the ensuing higher productivity may lead to greater profits and stock value. Providing a high level of customer service is also costly, but customer loyalty and firm reputation may benefit a company for years into the future. Employees and customers are examples of a company's stakeholders. Other stakeholders include suppliers, debtholders, local communities, and governments. What are a firm's obligations to these stakeholders? Some firms believe that they have a responsibility to their stakeholders and even to society at large. Although socially responsible firms seek both profit and purpose, others focus only on profit. Sustainable investors need to distinguish between the two.

Many companies have vast amounts of wealth and cash flow. They have the power to make positive changes in society. Indeed, the international nature of companies like Starbucks, Microsoft, and Disney often enables them to tackle global problems better than government organizations. But today, socially responsible companies are expected to be *woke*. Being woke means being aware of social issues and movements against injustice, inequality, and prejudice. A woke company supports movements fighting against social injustice. One example of how wokeness can also be profitable is Nike's social justice marketing campaign featuring Colin Kaepernick. This former football quarterback refused to stand for the national anthem in protest of police brutality. Nike's stock initially declined after the advertisement's airing, but the immediate surge in online sales convinced investors that it would have a positive impact on profits, and so its stock price rebounded.

This chapter explores the methods by which companies can be socially responsible. Donating to charitable causes is good. Enabling employees to donate and volunteer at philanthropic causes through matching programs is even better. Actively fighting against social injustice, pollution, and climate change helps everyone. But this chapter is also about you. How do you feel about a firm's environmental, social, and governance (ESG) activities? There are always trade-offs. For example, consider a transportation firm that is on the front lines in society against social injustice. But transportation companies use considerable oil. Thus, some would consider the firm as a polluter. Does a positive ESG activity get canceled by a negative ESG activity? Only you, the investor, can make that decision. This chapter describes the activities firms engage in to be socially responsible. Then, Chapter 3 helps you frame your value system so that you can better answer these questions.

What is corporate social responsibility?

Corporate social responsibility (CSR), also called *corporate citizenship*, is a business model in which a firm is socially and environmentally accountable to its stockholders, employees, community, other stakeholders, and society. This view differs dramatically from the purely capitalist model in which a business is responsible only to its owners—the stockholders. The CSR company recognizes that it can affect areas of society, including economic, social, and environmental aspects, and is determined to make a positive impact.

A CSR company can positively affect society through its ordinary business and special CSR programs, philanthropy, and volunteer efforts. Through its routine business operations, a CSR firm can reduce its pollution, build a strong bond with its employees, produce safe products, operate ethically, and more, all while providing jobs and economic growth through a well-run business. If done well, the company benefits society while boosting its brand and customer loyalty.

A company can also influence other firms for society's benefit. For example, many viewed the Washington Redskins, the National Football League (NFL) football team in Washington, DC, as having a racist name that offended Native Americans. In 2020, various companies financially pressured the team to change its name. FedEx, the shipping giant, signed a $205 million stadium naming rights deal with the Washington Redskins in 1999. On July 2, 2020, FedEx notified the team that it would remove its signage from the stadium after the NFL's 2020 season, six years before the deal's expiration, unless the team changed its name. Several retail outlets, like Amazon, Nike, Target, and Walmart, stopped selling Redskins merchandise. As a result of these pressures, the team stopped using the Redskins name and logo in 2020.

> "The emphasis placed by more and more companies on corporate social responsibility symbolises the recognition that prosperity is best achieved in an inclusive society."
>
> —Tony Blair

Traditionally, a company has been accountable to shareholders for its economic success. As CSR has evolved, the concept of accountability has become more prevalent. Firms provide quarterly and annual reports to detail that financial success. They can also be accountable to themselves and their shareholders regarding CSR activities. A good CSR firm is likely to have sustainability and community welfare goals that are specific and measurable. Annual reporting illustrates progress toward those goals.

An excellent example of such reporting occurs at Starbucks. Its 2019 Global Social Impact Report states that Starbucks reached its important milestones of producing ethically sourced coffee, creating a global network of farmers, contributing millions of hours of community service, and pioneering green buildings throughout its stores. Its CSR goals for 2020 and beyond include reducing its cups' environmental impact and hiring 10,000 refugees.

What is business ethics?

At one time, many considered "business ethics" an oxymoron—two words that just don't go together. A more common phrase to describe business morality was *caveat emptor*, which means buyer beware. Business ethics examines the ethical and moral principles in business activities. These norms and values guide a company in all aspects of commerce that it conducts.

> "Ethics is the new competitive environment."
> —Peter Robinson

Many firms have a Code of Conduct or Ethics to guide their employees' and managers' ethical behavior. For example, Amazon's Code of Business Conduct and Ethics directs employees to follow applicable laws, rules, and regulations. Amazon also provides specific directions in several areas.

- *Conflicts of interest.* A conflict of interest arises when an employee's interests conflict with the company's best interests.

- *Insider trading.* The company's employees aren't permitted to trade in stocks or other securities while possessing material nonpublic information. They may not pass on material nonpublic information to others without express company authorization or recommend that others trade in stock or other securities based on material nonpublic information.
- *Discrimination and harassment.* Amazon doesn't tolerate any illegal discrimination or harassment of any kind.
- *Health and safety.* Each employee is responsible for maintaining a safe and healthy workplace. The company doesn't permit violence and threatening behavior.
- *Price fixing.* Employees may not discuss prices with any competitor with which Amazon competes, where the result of such discussion would be inconsistent with antitrust laws.
- *Bribery and payments to government personnel.* Employees may not bribe anyone for any reason.
- *Recordkeeping, reporting, and financial integrity:* Amazon's public financial reports must contain full, fair, accurate, timely, and understandable disclosure as required by law.

Intel's Code of Conduct includes additional categories like being a responsible corporate citizen and conducting business with customers. The Code of Conduct for Alphabet (the parent company of Google) includes financial integrity and responsibility categories. In short, both business leaders and sustainable investors have recognized that ethical behavior can help companies maintain a better connection with their stakeholders.

Who are a firm's stakeholders?

Traditionally, the United States' corporate perspective has been that a firm's primary goal is to create wealth for its owners. For a public firm, the stockholders are the owners. This frame has driven corporate governance laws and policies about incentive structures for managers and monitoring systems to protect shareholders. However, many people believe that companies should have a greater responsibility to society than this narrow focus. This *stakeholder* view describes a firm as having many different groups with legitimate interests in its activities.

A company interacts with many people, groups, and institutions through its operation. By creating positive relationships with these stakeholders, a firm can create sus-

> "Business has a responsibility beyond its basic responsibility to its shareholders; a responsibility to a broader constituency that includes its key stakeholders: customers, employees, NGOs, government—the people of the communities in which it operates."
>
> —Courtney Pratt

tainable economic wealth. Many categorize stakeholders by how closely they interact with the firm. Consider the stakeholder bullseye diagram shown in Figure 2.1. The inner circle represents those stakeholders closest to the firm. These primary stakeholders include employees, managers, and shareholders (investors). In the next ring of the bullseye, secondary stakeholders (customers, suppliers, and creditors) are involved in the firm's economic transactions. This diagram's outer ring represents the tertiary stakeholders who have little direct engagement with the firm but still have a stake in its activities. These stakeholders could include the government (local and national), communities, labor unions, competitors, environment industry trade groups, and society.

The government receives taxes and fees from companies and, in many cases, regulates them. Local communities benefit from a firm's philanthropy and may suffer pollution created by the firm. A labor union, which influences the quality and tone of the employee–firm relationship, may represent a firm's employees. Competitors, industry trade groups, and other organizations within a company's industry are interested in the firm's activities. Many even consider the public, or society, a stakeholder.

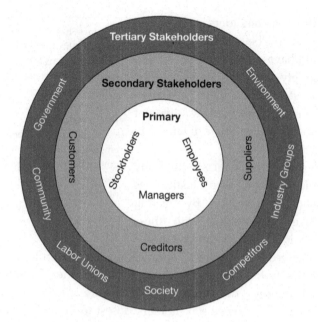

Figure 2.1 Firm Stakeholders

This stakeholder perspective directs firm executives to manage relations with each stakeholder group. Instead of maximizing stockholder wealth, this view aims to maximize sustainable organizational wealth by optimizing these relationships. Many companies now have an organizational unit, like a "sustainability group" or "corporate social responsibility committee," tasked with communicating with stakeholders.

How can a firm demonstrate its social responsibility?

CSR consists of three main categories: environmental, social, and governance (ESG).

- *Environmental.* The concept of environmental responsibility has evolved. Initially, it focused on pollution and depletion of natural resources. Recently, CSR advocates have combined these factors into an overall concern over climate change.

- *Social.* The social category focuses on the treatment of people within the firm and throughout society. Social responsibility could include diversity in employment recruiting policies, employee health and welfare, and product safety within the firm. A firm can be aware of how its operations affect local communities, protect animal welfare, and advocate for human rights. An emerging issue is the sustainability of a firm's supply chain. In the past, a firm might claim that it reduced its pollution level after closing its manufacturing plants and outsourcing production. However, contracting with suppliers in countries with weak environmental laws and enforcement typically adds to global pollution. Today, sustainability proponents include the ESG risks of a company's supply chain when assessing a company. Thus, firms need to ensure that their suppliers avoid inhumane practices, uphold environmental standards, and avoid child labor.

> "We know that the profitable growth of our company depends on the economic, environmental, and social sustainability of our communities across the world. And we know it is in our best interests to contribute to the sustainability of those communities."
>
> —Travis Engen

- *Governance. Corporate governance* refers to the mechanisms used to manage a corporation. Responsible corporate governance practices could involve using an independent auditor to review the accounting statements and records, utilizing a knowledgeable and independent board of directors, and paying reasonable executive compensation.

How can firms be environmentally sustainable?

To enhance environmental sustainability, companies can eliminate waste and emissions in their operations and minimize

> "A nation that destroys its soils destroys itself. Forests are the lungs of our land, purifying the air and giving fresh strength to our people."
> —Franklin D. Roosevelt

those practices that negatively affect the world's natural resources. CSR firms should follow all environmental laws. More importantly, companies can incorporate sustainable activities in various areas of activity, including waste management, energy efficiency, transportation, and sustainable procurement.

- Sustainable *waste management* involves minimizing waste and disposal to both pollute less and use fewer natural resources. For example, firms can use recycled products like paper and even go paperless when possible. More dramatically, firms can minimize the environmental impact of their production waste. Ben & Jerry's, a Vermont company that manufactures ice cream, frozen yogurt, and sorbet, is well known for pioneering creative ways to minimize its environmental footprint. The firm sends dairy waste from its ice cream production to a farm that uses it to generate biomass energy to power the farm.
- *Energy efficiency* can come in many forms. Nonmanufacturing companies like banks can use energy-efficient office buildings to keep them at an optimal temperature through innovations in insulation, airtight building material, and ventilation. Manufacturing firms can reduce their carbon footprint by using renewable energy, where possible, and production processes that capture pollution emissions.
- *Transportation systems* account for about a fifth of world energy consumption and carbon emission, thus contributing to climate change. The transportation of products, materials, and people is essential in business activity. The mode of transportation (land, water, and air) and its energy source determine the pollution caused. Companies can limit carbon emissions through sustainable transportation systems.
- *Sustainable procurement practices* refer to demanding socially responsible behavior from a firm's supply chain. That is, a

CSR firm can't skirt strict environmental laws in its home country by moving production to countries with weak environmental regulations. However, a non-CSR firm may be able to move the dirty part of its manufacturing to emerging markets by opening a factory or contracting a local firm to produce the products. Although these actions would be legal, they wouldn't be consistent with environmental sustainability and CSR.

How do firms demonstrate social responsibility to society?

The social aspect focuses on the treatment and freedom of people. In many cases, these are the people in the firm's local community. In other cases, firms focus on the plight of people suffering throughout the world. For example, in its value statements, Ben & Jerry's Homemade Holdings Inc. vows: "To operate the Company in a way that actively recognizes the central role that business plays in society by initiating innovative ways to improve the quality of life locally, nationally, and internationally." Some of the company's initiatives are racial justice, democracy, recognition of small-scale farmers in developing countries, LGBTQ+ equality, and support of refugees. The firm supports these causes through donations to national and international organizations dedicated to these issues.

Starbucks Coffee is known for its social impact mission, which it accomplishes through its business activities and investments. For example, the company supports ethically and responsibly produced coffee, tea, and cocoa, using education and resources through its support centers in coffee-producing countries worldwide. It also directly finances small-scale farms to allow them to renovate their farms for more sustainable practices. Another example is how Starbucks executes its hiring policies. Specific goals focus on hiring more at-risk youth, refugees, veterans, and military spouses and creating a generally diverse workforce.

> "A good company offers excellent products and services. A great company also offers excellent products and services but also strives to make the world a better place."
>
> —Philip Kotler

The Disney Company is known for several socially responsible programs. For example, in partnership with the Make-A-Wish Foundation, Disney helps fulfill more than 10,000 wishes annually for children battling life-threatening illnesses. Many recognize Disney for its support of volunteerism. The company encourages its employees to volunteer in their local communities and provides free theme park tickets to anyone who volunteers their time participating in nonprofit organizations.

Companies can also engage with the local communities in which they operate. Common examples include supporting a local charity, sponsoring a sports team or league, organizing clean-up events, sponsoring a local event, and helping local schools and community projects. Participating in these activities makes sense from both an ESG and commercial perspective. The more positive interactions a firm has with its stakeholders, the more likely it will be successful.

Overall, sustainable investors recognize that many companies display their values through efforts to help people's lives. A company can accomplish its value goals through its business operations and the social issues it supports through its charitable donations.

What firm governance characteristics are responsible?

Most large corporations have a separation between firm ownership and controls. Specifically, stockholders own the firm but have little control over it. The executives may or may not have much ownership but control the firm's activities. How can the stockholders (the *principals*) ensure that the executives (the *agents*) manage the firm for the owners' benefit? This situation is called the *principal-agent problem*. The stockholders desire profits and increasing stock prices, while other motives such as high compensation and additional perks may drive the executives. *Corporate governance* is the set of controls and incentives necessary to align the executives' interests with stockholders.

Corporate control rests with the executives and the board of directors. Stockholders elect the directors to guard their interests. Theoretically, the board should hold most of the power because it hires the executives and determines the executive compensation plans. In practice, the chief executive officer (CEO) often has power because the CEO influences those elected to the board. To maintain a board's independence from the CEO, socially responsible companies want a diverse board with most outside directors not connected to the CEO. They usually strive to select someone other than the CEO to be the board chairperson.

To help align the executive interests with those of the stockholders, the board can provide a compensation scheme in which executive pay varies depending on the firm's success. Because the stockholders want growing profits and an increasing stock price, the company rewards executives with higher compensation when these events occur. Several mechanisms are available for rewarding executives, like giving them a fixed number of shares that vest sometime in the future. Another method is to provide them with the right to buy shares at a fixed price, usually through stock options. Either way, the executives are likely to work hard and make decisions to raise the firm's stock price. Although these forms of equity compensation improve the alignment of executives' and stockholders' interests, these types of perks can create excessive compensation and lead to a general fairness controversy. Consider the following facts.

- In 2020, the average compensation for CEOs in the Standard & Poor's 500 Index (S&P 500) firms was $15.5 million.
- On average, CEOs of S&P 500 firms earned 299 times the average employee pay.

- McDonald's CEO earned 1,189.1 times its median paid employee.
- Paycom's Chad Richison made $211 million in 2020.
- Microsoft's Satya Nadella earned $44 million in 2020.
- Executives at JC Penney, Hertz, and Neiman Marcus received million-dollar bonuses in 2020 right before declaring bankruptcy and laying off tens of thousands of employees.

Given these facts, socially responsible companies try to align executive interests with stockholders without excessive and inequitable compensation.

How can firms exhibit social responsibility to employees?

Consider these two essential aspects of employee relations: treat employees well and motivate them with sustainable initiatives. The social part of CSR is about treating people well. Of course, a company's employees are the closest stakeholders to the firm. A CSR firm should ensure that its employees are happy and satisfied with their jobs. A company can't develop a reputation for social responsibility if it doesn't treat its employees well. Companies can improve their reputations by ensuring a safe work environment, paying fair compensation, and providing good benefits. Elite CSR firms go beyond traditional benefits and offer such things as:

- Providing inclusive health care policies like those that cover partners of LGBTQ+ employees,
- Offering scholarships to students who are the first in their families to go to college, and
- Investing in science, technology, engineering, and mathematics (STEM) education for daughters of employees.

People like working for a company that is trying to make the world a better place. Employees are more committed to their company when it focuses on CSR initiatives that they value. Such initiatives are vital for the millennial generation. When firms engage their employees in socially responsible initiatives, they find that employees have innovative ideas on positively affecting their community and meeting a business need. At the same time, savvy investors know that more committed employees are more productive. Thus, CSR initiatives can enhance company productivity. Indeed, academic studies show an association between employee satisfaction and extra stock returns, above the returns expected from their everyday business operations.

How can a firm be socially responsible in some areas and not in others?

Some firms can do only so much in all the ESG areas. Consider the oil and gas industry. The fossil fuels these firms produce are the primary source of carbon pollution, driving climate change concerns. Indeed, the production of a carbon energy source creates pollution. The occasional environmental disaster of oil spills such as *Deepwater Horizon* in the Gulf of Mexico and *Exxon Valdez* in Alaska's Prince William Sound also dramatically illustrates how negatively this industry can affect the environment.

Yet, oil companies engage in CSR initiatives in other areas. Oil companies like BP, ConocoPhillips, Shell, Total, and others have diverse workforces and pay employees well with high-quality benefits. They also spend billions of dollars each year developing lower carbon or "green" energy sources. These companies have active programs to support human rights, human development, and human freedom. For example, ConocoPhillips has diversity and inclusion goals that include actions like the following:

- Promote diversity and inclusion within its succession efforts.

- Improve the recruiting process to mitigate bias.
- Embed inclusion throughout the hiring process to attract a diverse candidate pool.
- Mandate diversity and inclusion goals for each business unit.
- Instill hiring managers and leaders with the skills, knowledge, and self-awareness to advance the firm's diversity efforts.
- Apply these high standards for diversity and inclusion throughout the supply chain.

Is ConocoPhillips a CSR firm? Each person who cares about CSR must assess whether the corporate citizenship activities in which big oil companies engage can compensate for their harm to the climate. People who have a passion for environmental sustainability tend to be critical of oil companies. Yet, those who have a passion for human rights and communities might place greater value on these firms' activities.

How does doing good differ from avoiding doing harm?

"Corporate social responsibility is not just about managing, reducing and avoiding risk. It is about creating opportunities, generating improved performance, making money and leaving the risks far behind."

—Suni Misser

Investors categorize CSR initiatives into activities related to avoiding socially irresponsible behavior versus actions taken to benefit society. Both are important, and yet they can require different levels of effort and intentions. For example, consider the banking industry. Banking isn't a polluting industry. Banks easily avoid polluting, but that doesn't impress anyone. Other than preventing harm, how can they do good in the environmental sustainability arena? One way is to use energy-efficient buildings. Saving energy reduces the bank's carbon footprint. However, a bolder action would be to stop financing oil, gas, and coal companies. In 2019, the top

35 banks funneled $735 billion to fossil fuel worldwide. Banks have been under social pressure to stop funding oil and coal since the 2016 signing of the Paris Agreement, whose central aim is to strengthen the global response to the threat of climate change. However, 20 of the 35 banks increased their financing levels from 2018 to 2019. This approach might be changing as Goldman Sachs announced at the end of 2019 that it would establish explicit restrictions on financing for any part of the oil-and-gas sector and rule out direct financing for thermal coal mines and coal-burning plants worldwide.

Another banking example is the treatment of animals. The operation of banks doesn't involve using animals; thus, it avoids animal cruelty claims. However, for 29 years, Wells Fargo sponsored Alaska's famous 1,000-mile dog-sled race, the Iditarod. In 2018, the bank decided it would no longer sponsor the event. Speculation was that outreach from the People for the Ethical Treatment of Animals (PETA) influenced the decision.

What is corporate philanthropy, and should firms be engaged in it?

The notion behind philanthropy entails driving social support and change through funding other organizations that focus on a particular issue, such as feeding the homeless, providing disaster relief, and offering child development. *Corporate philanthropy* is the act whereby a business promotes the welfare of others through charitable donations. Companies can achieve this objective by allowing employees to allocate contributions through their passion for social issues. In some cases, the company can determine the causes that it values.

The most popular form of corporate philanthropy is a matching gifts program. Firms match or sometimes double the donations made by employees. In this program, the

> "Philanthropy is not about the money. It's about using whatever resources you have at your fingertips and applying them to improving the world."
>
> —Melinda Gates

individual employee determines what charitable cause gets funded. A similar popular program involves the firm making contributions to charities where employees volunteer their time. For example, as an employee, when you volunteer for 20 hours or more, the firm contributes $500 to that nonprofit organization. A few companies have a substantial maximum of giving per employee match. For example, Microsoft has a maximum match of $15,000; Google's maximum match is $12,000; and Coca-Cola's is $20,000. Again, the employees determine where the corporate contributions go. The main advantages of these programs are that they allow companies to help their communities to enhance employee loyalty.

Companies also give directly to community causes, without employee contributions. These community grants support local nonprofits and community organizations to further their missions. Some companies fund a foundation for philanthropic giving. Consider that the

- Alcoa Foundation focuses on education and the environment.
- Coca-Cola Foundation focuses on female economic empowerment, clean water access, and active and healthy living.
- Duke Energy Foundation offers local community grants for education, economics and workforce development, and environment and community.
- Ford Motor Company Foundation funds grants in community life, education, and safety.
- Intel Foundation supports initiatives for science, technology, engineering, and math (STEM) education.
- Monsanto Fund supports nonprofit organizations in the areas of education, farming, gardening, robotics, and the arts.
- Safeway Foundation funds the four priority areas of hunger relief, education, health and human services, and assisting people with disabilities.

- United Health Foundation grants are primarily for community health, health education, and support for veterans.

From arts to veterans, the breadth of community and society causes supported by companies is quite large.

In return, the sponsored nonprofit acknowledges the support of these businesses in their events. Such programs also provide a positive public image because the firm's donations affect many different organizations. Sustainability investors know that corporate philanthropy is good business.

How can firms become involved in community engagement?

Companies can go beyond philanthropy with more pervasive and directed community engagement, also called *community involvement*. *Corporate community engagement* refers to a company's activities to enhance its contribution to the well-being of the communities in which it operates. While helping the community, it also improves the firm's reputation within the community. Firms can accomplish this goal through employee volunteer days, partnerships with local nonprofit organizations, and service-based organizations.

For example, United Parcel Service (UPS), an American multinational package delivery and supply chain management company, continues to deliver. In 2014, the CEO announced a goal to have 20 million employee volunteer hours by 2020. While employees volunteer their time at many community events, UPS also provides its logistics and transportation skillset. For example, UPS helps with recovery efforts after natural disasters, like Hurricane Florence in the United States and Typhoon Mangkhut in the Philippines. It also partners with organizations like the Boys & Girls Clubs of America and similar groups in other countries to educate young drivers on safe driving habits. These efforts strengthen the community and enhance the company's reputation.

Firms in the health care industry have used their expertise to end teenage smoking and educate children on healthy eating habits. UnitedHealth Group, an American for-profit managed health care company, donated money to help with the global impact of COVID-19 for urgent needs in the international communities where it operates. Also, by working with local nongovernmental organizations and public health systems, the UnitedHealth Group addresses the food insecurity, health care, and hygiene needs of vulnerable individuals and families. It also expands local health care system capacity through donations to community hospitals' intensive care units (ICUs) and regular beds.

Businesses can also withhold their business activity as a form of community engagement. For example, Major League Baseball (MLB) protested a newly passed voting law in Georgia by moving the 2021 MLB All-Star Game from Atlanta to Denver. MLB argued that the new law violated people's civil rights by restricting voting access for disadvantaged people. As a result, the Atlanta community lost millions of dollars of revenue from the event. Similar events have occurred. In 2017, the National Basketball Association (NBA) moved its All-Star Game out of Charlotte, North Carolina, because of a new 2016 law in North Carolina that required transgender people to use restrooms that correspond to their birth certificate sex designation. By withholding events like these, businesses and companies try to put economic pressure on communities and governments to improve civil and human rights.

"By working together to mobilize sustainable investment in the Least Developed Countries, government, business and civil society give hope and opportunity to the world's poorest."

—Kofi Annan

How can investors determine whether a firm is socially responsible?

The United Nations (UN) developed its Ten Principles of the United Nations Global Compact to partner with companies worldwide to uphold those principles. Many consider that the signatories to this initiative identify as socially responsible firms. The United Nations Global Compact webpages list the companies that have agreed to the compact. In early 2021, the UN's webpage listed more than 12,000 companies from over 160 countries. Searching for a company on the website is easy. However, even with such an extensive worldwide participant list, many prominent firms don't participate. More than half (17 out of 30) of the Dow Jones Industrial Average companies aren't listed. Table 2.1 presents the Ten Principles by category.

> "People are going to want, and be able, to find out about the citizenship of a brand, whether it is doing the right things socially, economically and environmentally."
>
> —Mike Clasper

Table 2.1 Ten Principles of the United Nations Global Compact

Businesses should follow certain principles:

Human Rights

Principle 1. Support and respect the protection of internationally proclaimed human rights.

Principle 2. Ensure that they are not complicit in human rights abuses.

Labor

Principle 3. Uphold the freedom of association and the effective recognition of the right to collective bargaining.

Principle 4. Support the elimination of all forms of forced and compulsory labor.

Principle 5. Back the effective abolition of child labor.

Principle 6. Support the elimination of discrimination in respect of employment and occupation.

Environment

Principle 7. Support a precautionary approach to environmental challenges.

Principle 8. Undertake initiatives to promote greater environmental responsibility.

Principle 9. Encourage the development and diffusion of environmentally friendly technologies.

Anticorruption

Principle 10. Work against corruption in all its forms, including extortion and bribery.

Most of these principles involve "avoiding harm" rather than "doing good." In that vein, you may want to know what risks a firm faces from ESG factors. How likely is a specific company to experience an environmental disaster? How likely is a firm to have public relations problems due to human rights issues? An ESG Risk Rating can help assess the extent to which a firm's value is at risk from ESG issues. Sustainalytics, Inc. produces these ratings (www.sustainalytics.com). You can also search for any company using the Yahoo! Finance website. You enter the company's ticker, such as BA for Boeing Company. When the stock quote information appears, click on the Sustainability link in the menu. The measures use a two-dimensional framework to assess a firm's exposure to industry-specific ESG risks and how well it manages those risks. Measuring the ESG Risk Scores involves a scale between 0 and 100, with a higher number indicating more risk.

Along with the ESG Risk Score number, the website provides a risk category to interpret that value. The risk-level categories include negligible, low, medium, high, or severe. Lastly, the ESG Risk Score is the sum of three risk scores that individually represent the risk level in ESG criteria. For example, Boeing, the airplane manufacturer, had an ESG Risk Score of 39 in mid-2020, categorized as high risk. As expected, some of this high value is because it is a multinational corporation that designs, manufactures, and sells airplanes, rotorcraft, rockets, satellites, telecommunications equipment, and missiles worldwide; and some of its products pollute. However, the more significant problem comes from a high Social Risk Score. Presumably, that is because of its problems with its Boeing 737 Max in 2019 and 2020.

Finally, a firm with good sustainability initiatives wants to communicate them to stakeholders. You can check the company's investor relations website for a CSR or sustainability report to get detailed information on its social responsibility. The firm may also follow the International Organization for Standardization (ISO) rules, specifically ISO 26000. The ISO creates international standards in such areas as technology, manufacturing, health, and safety. In 2010, ISO started ISO 26000 Guidance on Social Responsibility. If a firm mentions that it has adopted ISO 26000, then it is likely socially responsible.

How are firms held accountable for CSR?

Corporations provide quarterly financial reports and one annual report to detail the business activities and transactions that lead to their economic bottom lines. The Securities and Exchange Commission (SEC) and individual stock exchanges require these reports. No similar required report is available for ESG activities.

> "Companies with their eye on their 'triple-bottom-line' outperform their less fastidious peers on the stock market."
> —*The Economist*

However, firms can hold themselves CSR accountable. They can create annual sustainability or CSR reports to be transparent about those activities. Reporting on the economic bottom line and activities to support the environment and society is the *triple-bottom-line report*. Although standards are available for the financial report, like generally accepted accounting principles (GAAP), no standards are available for reporting CSR activities. However, some best practices exist. For example, a sustainability report should state a firm's specific goals, indicate its methods for measuring progress, and demonstrate that progress. For example, IKEA, the Swedish multinational group that designs and sells ready-to-assemble furniture, kitchen appliances, and home accessories, has a Chief Sustainability Officer and produces an annual summary of sustainability activities. A few of the most critical areas to IKEA concern community involvement, employee well-being, diversity and inclusion, greenhouse gas emissions, air pollution, human rights, and water stewardship.

IKEA lays out specific goals. For example, by 2025, the firm wants to include in its supply chain products or services

"Without reliable climate-related financial information, financial markets cannot price climate-related risks and opportunities correctly and may potentially face a rocky transition to a low-climate economy."

—Michael Bloomberg

made by local social businesses in all the countries in which they operate. A *social business*, also known as a *social entrepreneur*, is a business that has specific social objectives that serve its primary purposes, like supporting women, migrants, and those with disabilities. By 2019, IKEA had partnered with 32 social businesses in 16 countries. Another example is IKEA's goal to support refugees by setting up centers for employment skills training. By 2022, the firm aims to have 300 such refugee training facilities worldwide. IKEA's sustainability report is good because it sets forth specific goals, a timeframe for achieving them, and metrics measuring progress.

Although no formal process exists for publicly tracking and reporting progress on CSR goals, the media and nonprofit organizations closely watch them. However, CSR progress success only matters if investors hold companies accountable by owning or avoiding their stock.

What is a nongovernmental organization, and how does it interact with companies?

A *nongovernmental organization* (NGO), also known as a *civil society organization*, is a nonprofit group that operates independently from for-profit businesses and governments. Each NGO brings people and groups together regarding societal initiatives organized around a particular social or political purpose. The Red Cross, Habitat for Humanity, American Heart Association, and Greenpeace are well-known NGOs. NGOs are not public corporations and thus don't issue stock.

NGOs consist of two types: operational NGOs and advocacy NGOs. An operational NGO focuses on designing and implementing development-related projects like animal species recovery and protection. Within the advocacy category, an NGO tends to engage in watchdog campaigns or social movement campaigns. For a watchdog campaign, the goal is to pressure the targeted firms or politicians to comply with the NGO's goal.

> "If we all act together—business, governments, NGOs and citizens and, especially, the young—just imagine the good we could create."
>
> —Paul Polman

Industry watchdogs are commonly concerned with broader policy and business environment issues in which the product or service exists. Consumer-focused watchdogs like *Consumer Reports* are concerned with product safety, price competition, quality, and truth in advertising. Large advocacy groups like AARP, a U.S.-based interest group focusing on issues affecting those over 50, advocate for a group of people through consumer-focused activities and political lobbying. Groups in the social movement advocacy category attempt to change some parts of society. Well-known examples are Mothers Against Drunk Driving (MADD), Dreamers, and Earth Watch.

For more than two decades, the Carbon Disclosure Project (CDP) has provided a global disclosure system for investors, companies, cities, states, and regions to manage their environmental impacts. The CDP believes that people must act urgently to prevent dangerous climate change and environmental damage. Its role is to provide transparency and environmental impact measures for 9,600 companies globally and over 800 cities, states, and regions worldwide. CDP publicly reports letter grades A, A–, B, B–, C, C–, D, and D– in the three categories of climate change, forests, and water security. Table 2.2 shows the 2020 scores for various companies.

Through these ratings, companies and communities can gauge their progress on these critical environmental issues. Interestingly, Philip Morris International, a tobacco company, has the best scores of the companies listed above. This finding illustrates that a firm producing a socially problematic product may perform well in other socially responsible areas.

Table 2.2 Carbon Disclosure Scores for Various Companies

Company	Climate Change	Water Security	Forests
Ashland Global Holdings	D	D	C
Coca-Cola Company	A–	A–	D
Hershey Company	C	C	B–
Kellogg	B	B	B
Philip Morris International	A	A	A
Tyson Foods	B–	A–	C
Walmart	A	C	C

These NGOs are important to companies for two main reasons. First, a CSR firm may want to link with local or national NGOs to champion specific societal goals. Nonprofit organizations like the American Cancer Society have many corporate partners. The NGO gets funding, and the company gains a positive reputation for socially responsible philanthropy. The other interaction with NGOs can be damaging. Watchdog groups publicize a firm's irresponsibility, like polluting a river or poor treatment of people along its supply chain. A socially responsible firm should minimize the watchdog impact by working with the group to resolve potential problems.

How can a firm have a social purpose and earn a profit?

The traditional finance view is that a firm cannot maximize its profits over time when distracted by noneconomically focused activities. Conducting socially driven activities takes resources. A more socially responsible company may decide to reallocate a substantial portion of cash toward philanthropy, capital investment, personnel costs, and management time. Yet, a firm needs those resources to be successful in its product markets. Otherwise, better economically focused competitors are likely to gain some of its customers.

However, CSR advocates suggest that a firm can earn a profit and achieve social goals. How do they do it? Firms can be strategic in determining which social activities they perform. For example, they can choose those activities that are more easily integrated into their operations and communicated within a firm's differentiation strategy. The social activities can even bind the company more tightly to its employees, customers, and other stakeholders. Well-run, socially responsible efforts can lead to:

> "Corporate Social Responsibility is a hard-edged business decision. Not because it is a nice thing to do or because people are forcing us to do it because it is good for our business."
> —Niall FitzGerald

- Higher employee morale and lower turnover,
- More talented employees and managers,
- Increased productivity,
- Higher sales,
- Lower litigation risk,
- Additional investors, and
- Higher stock price.

Social responsibility may sometimes cost a little more but can prevent costly crisis events. Being socially responsible is like buying homeowners insurance: it costs money but can avoid a devastating financial loss if a fire occurs. For example, a firm's supply chain that inhumanely treats workers may provide products at a lower cost. Eventually, advocacy groups and the media are likely to find out. Thus, the negative publicity may turn off many consumers, lead to boycotts, and reduce sales. Lower sales and the ensuing long-term effort to repair its image would cost the firm much more than paying only a little more for a more sustainable supply chain.

Consider Volkswagen (VW), a German automaker. It had a good reputation for being a socially responsible company. VW

> "It takes 20 years to build a reputation and five minutes to ruin it."
>
> —Benjamin Franklin

makes high-quality, environmentally friendly cars with safety as a priority. The Dow Jones Sustainability Index crowned Volkswagen as the industry leader for sustainability in the auto sector. In 2015, the U.S. Environmental Protection Agency (EPA) announced that VW had intentionally programmed diesel engines to activate their emissions controls during emissions testing. This action caused a vehicle's nitrogen oxide emissions output to meet U.S. standards during required testing while emitting up to 40 times more in real-world driving. That is, instead of investing in technology to meet emissions standards, VW simply cheated. The scandal cost VW over $33 billion in fines and financial settlements. The lost reputation also caused a reduced demand for the company's cars.

How is CSR viewed around the world?

> "CSR is not a static concept—it is a moving, evolving target."
>
> —Norine Kennedy

CSR has become internationally popular over the past few decades. One gauge of this popularity is the number of international organizations that issue sustainability goals with some business aspects. For example, the United Nations developed its Millennium Development Goals (MDGs) with corporate responsibility implications. A total of 191 UN members endorsed the MDGs. The World Health Organization (WHO) sponsored the World Summit on Sustainable Development. The Organization for Economic Cooperation and Development (OECD) advocates for better governance among its member countries and guides an international business through the OECD Guidelines for Multinational Enterprises. The Guideline is a code of conduct for environmental management, human rights, anticorruption, and supply chain management.

CSR and ESG are likely the most popular in Europe. The European Union's European Commission (EC) has enacted several sustainability initiatives. In 2019, the EC proposed its Green Deal, a strategy and action plan to transform the European Union (EU) into a resource-efficient and competitive economy. Its general goals are to achieve no net emissions of greenhouse gasses by 2050, decouple economic growth from resource use, and leave no person or place behind. In support of the European Green Deal, the EC has a workstream that it summarizes as sustainable finance, guiding private investment in transitioning to a climate-neutral economy. Examples of the workflow include giving companies guidance on reporting their business's climate impacts and disclosure obligations for financial products like bonds.

Companies in China have made substantial strides in incorporating ESG factors into their decision making but still lag their Western counterparts. Although the number of company CSR reports has risen, the portion considered of good quality has declined. The listed state-owned companies are more likely to incorporate and report on the government's ESG priorities, like pollution control and alleviation of poverty. ESG reporting in China may expand considerably. Although Chinese regulators, the China Securities Regulatory Commission, and China's Ministry of Environmental Protection planned to introduce mandatory ESG disclosures for listed companies by the end of 2020, the expected date is now 2021 or later due to the pandemic.

What companies are known as leaders in CSR?

Thus far, companies mentioned as leaders in CSR include Alphabet (Google), Amazon, Ben & Jerry's, Coca-Cola, Disney, IKEA, Intel, Microsoft, Nike, Starbucks, Target, UnitedHealth Group, UPS, and Walmart. However, as the VW story illustrates, a company can be considered ESG focused until some event or private information is revealed. Thus, sustainable investors need to keep up with society's view of each company.

Nevertheless, here are some other companies known for their sustainability and responsibility efforts:

- Patagonia, an outdoor clothing retailer, gives 1% of all sales to environmental organizations globally and considers itself an activist company.
- Warby Parker makes and sells eyewear. When a customer buys a pair of glasses, the firm distributes a second pair to someone in need.
- TOMS, a shoe company, has an active social agenda and pledges to donate at least one-third of its annual net profits to those causes.
- LEGO, a toy company, is committed to providing children from all backgrounds access to play. It's moving toward more sustainable energy sources in its manufacturing and office buildings.
- Novo Nordisk, a pharmaceutical company, is transitioning to a zero environmental impact business model.
- Levi Strauss, an American clothing company, prides itself on taking courageous stands to help fuel social movements.
- GlaxoSmithKline is committed to reducing its environmental footprint and reducing waste and emissions by 25% by 2030.
- Bosch dedicates half of its research and development budget to creating technology that protects the environment.

Others include 3M, Apple, Bridgestone, Canon, Cisco, Dell, Estée Lauder, Michelin, Sony, and Toyota.

What online resources are available for researching socially responsible firms?

Here are some websites that provide information about CSR and ESG.

- Yahoo! Finance reports sustainability metrics for each company: https://finance.yahoo.com
- AFL-CIO Executive Paywatch reports on executive pay each year: https://aflcio.org/paywatch
- Double the Donation reports on corporate philanthropy: https://doublethedonation.com/tips/corporate-philanthropy
- United Nations Global Compact details: https://www.unglobalcompact.org
- Components of the Dow Jones Sustainability Indices: https://www.spglobal.com/esg/csa/indices/djsi-index-family
- Sustainability Accounting Standards Board has reporting standards for U.S. companies: https://www.sasb.org
- Global Reporting Initiative has reporting standards for international companies: https://www.globalreporting.org/Pages/default.aspx
- Certified B Corporations are businesses verified to meet a set of criteria and balance profit and purpose: https://bcorporation.net/about-b-corps
- The Carbon Disclosure Project provides a comprehensive dataset on corporate and city environmental action: https://www.cdp.net/en

Takeaways

CSR is a company initiative that ensures it uses its resources to create positive change in the community and worldwide. Sustainable investors look for firms with activities in ESG. Here are some essential lessons from this chapter.

- Search for firms with social goals that are specific and measurable.
- Look for firms that hold themselves accountable for their social goals.
- Review a firm's codes of conduct or ethics.

- Identify how a firm interacts with its stakeholders.
- Examine a firm's reaction to climate change.
- Avoid firms with excessive CEO compensation.
- Decide whether a firm needs to be responsible in all ESG areas or just some.
- Review the goals of a firm's philanthropic activities.
- Decide what community engagement initiatives are most important to you.
- Look for firms that choose social goals easily integrated into their operations to succeed in profit and purpose.

3

SOCIAL AND RELIGIOUS VALUES

ALIGNING VALUES AND PORTFOLIO ASSETS

> We can't save the world by playing by the rules, because the rules have to be changed. Everything needs to change—and it has to start today.
>
> —Greta Thunberg

The sustainable investing landscape has dramatically changed over the past 50 years. Public interest in ethical investment vehicles took off in 1971 as a reaction to the Vietnam War. Dissatisfaction with the war caused some investors to wonder how corporations used their capital for manufacturing weapons and Agent Orange, a chemical sprayed on Vietnamese jungles that caused deformities in the babies of people who encountered it. The launching of the Pax Fund accommodated these socially conscious investors. It focused on avoiding companies profiting from the war. Later, other mutual funds excluded companies producing products considered harmful to society and shunned firms profiting from doing business in countries with oppressive governments.

Today, the basis of sustainable investing is personal values. Personal values are just that—personal. One person's values can differ from those of another in both focus and conviction. Many people's values derive from strong beliefs stemming from religion, political association, and patriotism. They can target topics like social values, civil rights, and climate change. This chapter also discusses how some beliefs about what is socially sound can conflict between different value-based systems.

Values-based investing has become very popular. Since values differ among people, hundreds of investment opportunities are available through mutual funds and exchange-traded funds (ETFs) to serve different social investing goals. Instead of simply avoiding companies doing bad things, today's socially responsible investors often take a positive approach and seek to find companies doing good things. Sustainable investors need to reflect on their values and then assess which funds purport principles that match.

Social, political, and religious beliefs are the basis for most values-based investing. The key is to understand your values and the strength of your convictions. This chapter illustrates how different social, political, and religious beliefs lead to various views about investing. Thus, it will help you reflect on your values and demonstrate how investing can match your goals.

What is value-based investing?

Many investors don't pick their stocks based solely on expected risk and return and then fit them into a portfolio. In addition to risk and return factors, a growing number of investors seek companies that operate in a manner consistent with their beliefs. These beliefs are personal and can stem from patriotism, religion, environmental concerns, social values, civil rights, ethical values, and more. *Value-based investing* is an investment approach that considers the environmental and social impact of a company's actions, products, and leaders. It aligns your investment strategy with your ethics. However, people have very different moral passions. For example, one person may have a stronger inclination toward validating a given company as a steward of nature and ambassador for environmental sustainability. Another may place a higher priority on whether the firm supports human and civil rights.

Value-based beliefs are personal, and values differ. As such, people often have the opposite reaction to some topics. For example, consider companies that produce and sell firearms. For some people, excluding these firearm firms from their portfolios is paramount because they believe guns are harmful to society. Others are strong proponents of the Second Amendment to the U.S. Constitution, which gives citizens the right to bear arms. From this perspective, firearm firms support their rights, and thus such investors may want to include their stock in a portfolio. Or consider how a firm treats the partners of gay employees. Many proponents of human and civil rights advocate that firms treat gay partners like married spouses and offer them health benefits. Conversely, adherents to some religions oppose offering such benefits. These opposite values may determine who invests in a particular company.

Sustainable investors need to review their values and assess to what degree they should affect their investment strategy. For example, consider someone who believes alcohol is a menace to society. This person would choose not to own beer and liquor producers, like Anheuser-Busch, or alcohol distributors and stores. But how far should that ideal be taken? Alcohol makes up a small percentage of sales at grocery stores, restaurants, and convenience stores. Should sustainable investors consider avoiding investing in these companies too? Thus, sustainable investors must reflect on their values and the strength of their convictions. Many topics addressed in this chapter will help you reflect on popular values used in investment decision making.

What community values can investors use to select investments?

How well does a company support its local community? One way to assist a community is through charitable giving. For

> "Clients do not come first.
> Employees come first.
> If you take care of your
> employees, they will take
> care of the clients."
> —Richard Branson

example, companies sponsor youth sports teams, food drives, and wellness events like "walk for women" or a tree-planting campaign. Higher-level community engagement may support affordable housing, access to health care, and education. Companies may also match their employees' giving. Investors who value community engagement seek out companies serving their local communities. Alternatively, companies may create controversies within their communities, like having a history of involvement in land-use legal cases and egregiously negative community impacts from operations. Lastly, supporting a community also means the company pays its local, state, or national taxes. Paying taxes is essential to a community's health but is not necessarily consistent with minimizing costs and can contrast with a firm's profit-maximizing goal.

Some also consider employee relations a community issue as the employees likely live in the region. Are employees treated ethically and earning a living wage? Good treatment of employees includes working well with their union (if any), sharing any company profits through cash or option profit-sharing programs, having outstanding employee benefits, and having robust health and safety programs.

These community and employee values can vary between investors. Consider the Iditarod dog sled race in Alaska, nicknamed The Last Great Race. The annual 1,000-mile race honors the run to Nome that took place in 1925 to deliver serum to save the town from a developing epidemic. The race is a uniquely Alaskan cultural event. Alaskan Native history includes dog sled transportation. However, People for the Ethical Treatment of Animals (PETA) have long considered the race cruel to dogs. ExxonMobil was a sponsor of the Iditarod race since 1978 but dropped the sponsorship after the 2021 race due to public pressure from PETA. After discussions with PETA, Wells Fargo had previously dropped its sponsorship in

2017. Personal values on this issue likely determine whether you might invest in or shun ExxonMobil or Wells Fargo now that they are no longer Iditarod sponsors.

How can investing include human and civil rights values?

The protection of human rights is a critical issue for sustainable investors. Prohibiting child labor and providing humane working conditions are only the beginning. Respecting human rights can be shown in various ways. For example, a company can show respect for indigenous peoples' sovereignty, land, and culture. Sustainable investors avoid owning companies from countries with a history of human rights abuses, forced labor, and violation of free speech and other rights. Unfortunately, some companies can get tripped up through human rights violations in their supply chain. For example, consider a class action complaint against prominent electronics manufacturers stating that they benefited from young children in the Democratic Republic of Congo mining cobalt, a vital component of the rechargeable lithium-ion battery used in electronic devices. Some have accused well-known retailers of selling clothes produced in Bangladesh sweatshops. Often these cases end up having no legal consequences, but sustainable investors take note.

Some in the investment world characterize civil rights through corporate diversity and inclusion policies. Sustainable investors want to see women and minorities represented in leadership and board of directors positions. Also, what are the progressive policies regarding gay and lesbian employees? Progressive policies include providing benefits to employees' domestic partners, promoting diversity in the workforce, and supporting disability, racial, sexual orientation, and gender identity (LGBTQ+). Sustainable investors avoid firms with a record of affirmative action controversies.

"Injustice anywhere is a threat to justice everywhere."
—Martin Luther King Jr.

What is environmental sustainability, and how can investors incorporate it into a portfolio?

Climate change is currently the most popular environmental issue. However, before climate change subsumed environmental sustainability, many debated other noteworthy environmental topics in isolation, like air pollution, deforestation, and water/soil contamination. The term *climate change* in investing refers to the long-term change in weather patterns attributed to human causes. Activities like burning fossil fuels, cutting down rainforests, and farming certain livestock add enormous amounts of greenhouse gases to the atmosphere. Those greenhouse gases trap solar radiation, raising the planet's temperature and altering weather patterns. Traditionally, the economy depended on burning fossil fuels as the primary energy source to generate electricity, such as burning coal, oil, and natural gas. Also, fossil fuels run the transportation system to operate cars, trucks, trains, and airplanes. Lastly, fossil fuels power the manufacturing industry. Society needs to develop low-pollution and renewable sources of energy to combat climate change. Both governments and investors can foster this change. Governments can form policies and regulations to make carbon processes more expensive. The Paris Climate Agreement, adopted in 2015, provided some direction for governments. Another way to enhance the conversion to renewable energy is through the allocation of capital. That is, investors can reallocate capital from high carbon firms to low carbon and renewable energy firms. That is what investors do by making sustainable investments and forming sustainable portfolios.

> "Responding to climate change requires that we break every rule in the free-market playbook and that we do so with great urgency."
>
> —Naomi Klein

Sustainable investors seek firms generating or using renewable energy. The primary sources of renewable energy are solar, wind, hydropower, biomass, geothermal, or wave energy. Since fossil fuel-based transportation is a primary source of greenhouse gases, sustainable investors seek to support green transportation. This support includes the entire transportation value chain, from green vehicle production to green transportation infrastructure. Green investors also seek to avoid investing in fossil fuel energy production, namely, thermal coal extraction, thermal coal power generation, oil and gas production, and oil and gas power generation. However, the distinction between green and nongreen firms can be complicated. For example, Tesla produces electric cars, which are desirable for sustainable investors. However, Tesla uses enormous amounts of energy produced from fossil fuels to manufacture those cars, which is undesirable. Thus, its eco-friendly status is unclear.

Besides greenhouse gas emissions, sustainable investors are also concerned about air pollution, deforestation, and water and soil contamination. Chemical and industrial pollution are significant sources of water contamination. Examples of extreme disasters include:

- BP's *Deepwater Horizon* oil spill in the Gulf of Mexico in 2010,
- Kingston fossil plant coal fly ash spill in Tennessee in 2008,
- Chemical plant explosions in Jilin, China, in 2005,
- Baia Mare cyanide spill in Romania in 2000,
- *Exxon Valdez* oil spill in Prince William Sound in 1989, and
- Toxic gas leak from the Union Carbide (now Dow Chemical) pesticide plant in Bhopal, India in 1984.

Mainly because of these environmental disasters and many more minor incidents, investors concerned about the environment often avoid companies in the chemical industry in addition to the fossil fuel prohibition.

What products of firms are inconsistent with social responsibility?

The socially responsible movement began by avoiding investments in companies producing products deemed harmful for society or those benefiting from a government engaged in suppressing its population. This exclusion strategy centered on companies operating in South Africa or producing alcohol, gambling, tobacco, firearms, weapons (military), or nuclear power. Some investors were boycotting South Africa because of its apartheid regime that mandated state-sanctioned racial segregation. As a result, they avoided companies doing business in South Africa. The economic pressure from this boycott highlighted to the African leaders the extent of international opposition to the government, which contributed to the eventual dissolution of apartheid in 1994. Later, socially responsible investors no longer excluded companies doing business in South Africa from their portfolios.

A shift in thinking has occurred about nuclear power. Nuclear power was considered harmful for society because of the human and environmental toll from several accidents and many near misses. The best-known incidents were in Chernobyl (Ukraine), Three Mile Island (United States), and Fukushima (Japan). However, other incidents occurred in many other countries, including Czechoslovakia, France, Germany, Hungary, Spain, Sweden, Switzerland, and the United Kingdom. Also, over the decades, people have realized that nuclear energy is low cost, has zero carbon emissions, can produce high amounts of power, and is reliable when operated safely. Thus, many sustainable investors prefer nuclear energy generation over coal- and oil-based energy plants. Therefore, nuclear power is no longer on many exclusion lists.

What religious values affect investing?

Religious ideologies are essential values on which to base investment principles for believers. Indeed, socially responsible investing has its roots in religious values. The early days of SRI mainly consisted of investing in a manner consistent with one's morals. For example, the Religious Society of Friends (Quakers), at the Quaker

"My financial adviser says I don't have enough faith, and my spiritual adviser says I'm too diversified."
—Brad Fitzpatrick (cartoon)

Philadelphia Yearly Meeting in 1758, decreed that members were prohibited from participating in the slave trade. One of the Methodist Church founders, John Wesley, outlined "The Use of Money" in the late 1700s. His fundamental social investing principles were to avoid harming one's neighbors through business practices and to avoid industries like tanning and chemical production that can harm workers' health. Investors implemented these early origins of sustainable investing by screening companies that make products deemed harmful to society. Many refer to companies having anything to do with making alcohol, tobacco, gambling, pornography, and weapons as enterprises dealing in "sin stocks." Such a designation implies a religious connotation.

Attitudes about these "sins" differ between religious denominations. For example, historically, primarily Muslims and Mormons discouraged using tobacco. Society's general opposition to tobacco started in the 1950s when scientific evidence revealed its health risks. Social progressives who emphasize health promoted the shunning of tobacco stocks. Practicing Mormons, Assemblies of God parishioners, and Muslims adhere to their faith's stricture against drinking alcohol, but few Jews, Episcopalians, and Catholics identify alcohol as a sin. Protestant and Mormon faiths discourage gambling, but many Catholics and Jews view it as an acceptable activity. Indeed, Catholic churches have long been known for holding bingo events. Because of these differences, faith-based investing can occur through specific programs or mutual funds aligned with their religion's investment restrictions.

How can investors consider Christian values?

Christian faith-based investing stems from religious investment restrictions and advocating for investment in firms that promote social good. However, given the many Christian ideologies, different views exist on matching religious values and investments.

Many investment vehicles target Roman Catholics. Some of these policies follow those described by the United States Conference of Catholic Bishops (USCCB). The following six principles outline these policies.

- *Protecting human life.* The USCCB investment policy prescribes the absolute exclusion of investment in companies whose activities include direct participation in or support of abortion. Other prohibitions include investing in companies that manufacture contraceptives and engage in embryonic stem cell research and human cloning.
- *Promoting human dignity.* USCCB investment policies encourage companies to respect fundamental human rights, especially in countries with documented practices that violate their citizens' human rights. In addition, these policies advocate for equal opportunities for women and minorities. Finally, investors should avoid participation in investments related to pornography.
- *Reducing arms production.* USCCB investment policy avoids firms primarily engaged in military weapons manufacturing, including the production of antipersonnel landmines and the development of biological, chemical, or nuclear weapons.
- *Pursuing economic justice.* USCCB advocates avoiding the use of sweatshops for manufacturing goods, but it promotes generous wages and benefits and worker safety. With regard to the discriminatory practice of *redlining*, which denies access to credit in disadvantaged neighborhoods, USCCB doesn't deposit funds in

a financial institution that receives a poor rating from federal regulatory agencies under the Community Reinvestment Act.

- *Protecting the environment.* USCCB investment policy encourages corporations to preserve the planet's ecological legacy while addressing the widespread poverty in the poorest nations. It also encourages business initiatives for energy conservation and the development of alternate renewable and clean energy resources.
- *Encouraging corporate responsibility.* USCCB encourages companies to report on social and environmental performance. It also promotes and supports shareholder resolutions directed toward adopting corporate social responsibility guidelines.

Standard and Poor's launched an index in 2015, the S&P 500 Catholic Values Index (Ticker: SPXCVUT), which begins with the 500 stocks in the S&P 500 Index and excludes those with activities that lack alignment with USCCB investment policies. The Global X S&P 500 Catholic Values ETF (CATH) is an exchange-traded fund (ETF) linked to this index. Other popular Catholic values-focused investments are the Ave Maria Mutual Funds, Knights of Columbus Mutual Funds, and many investment advisory firms.

> "No one can serve two masters. Either you will hate the one and love the other, or you will be devoted to the one and despise the other. You cannot serve both God and money."
>
> —Matthew 6:24

The Church of Jesus Christ of Latter-day Saints, popularly known as the Mormon Church, doesn't provide direct investment advice to parishioners. However, the church's investment fund started reporting quarterly holdings to the Securities and Exchange Commission (SEC) in 2020. At first glance, the stocks held within their $37.8 billion fund may seem like any traditional investment fund. However, the stocks excluded from the portfolio are very revealing. For example, the church counsels its members not to consume tobacco, alcohol, or hot caffeinated drinks. It purposefully omits caffeinated sodas from its list of acceptable products within its health code. Consistent with these beliefs, the portfolio shows no investments in cigarette or beer manufacturers, coffee chains, Coca-Cola, PepsiCo, or Keurig Dr Pepper.

The American Baptist Home Mission Society revised its "Guidelines Relating to Social Criteria for Investments" in 2016. The Guidelines align investment decisions with concerns about long-term stability, social values, respect for human rights, social justice, and God's creation and environmental justice. In this regard, the principles exclude investments that derive 10% or more of revenues in the following:

- production, distribution, or sales of products that are in the tobacco, gambling, or liquor business,
- production, distribution, or sales of products that are pornographic, obscene, or harmful to minors, and
- production of nuclear, chemical, or biological weapons systems or firearms.

How can investors consider Islamic values?

Investors incorporate Islamic principles into investing through halal investment practices. The term *halal* means "permissible." Thus, halal investing complies with Shariah law, the canonical law of Islam. Some refer to halal investing as Shariah-compliant investing. The important investing principles of halal investing require the following:

- prohibition of *riba* (exploitative gains),
- prohibition of *gharar* (chance or gambling),
- avoidance of *haram* (forbidden) businesses or industries,
- ban on hoarding gold and silver, and
- sharing of profit.

The prohibition of riba is best known as a ban on paying or receiving interest. However, the mandate is more encompassing than that. It means the growth of money by the mere passage of time or increased capital without providing any services from an investing perspective. This prohibition makes banking at traditional Western banks difficult because halal investing excludes money market accounts, certificates of deposit, and other interest-bearing services. It also affects traditional asset allocation and diversification by excluding fixed-income securities like municipal bonds, U.S. Treasuries, and corporate bonds. The prohibition of riba also influences stock investing. Although riba permits owning company stock, it doesn't allow holding companies that pay or receive substantial amounts of interest. Thus, halal investing bans owning the stock of Western banks and companies with high amounts of debt. How much debt is too much? The Accounting and Auditing Organization for Islamic Financial Institutions (AAOIFI) issues halal security selection guidelines. Per AAOIFI guidelines, the debt limits are debt ratios of 30%, accounts receivables ratios of 45%, and interest income of 5%.

> "But Allah has permitted trade and has forbidden interest."
> —Quran 2:275

The prohibition of gharar also has important investment implications. Gharar doesn't permit investing in companies that profit from chance or gambling. Although a ban on owning casino-type companies is apparent, a ban on owning insurance companies may not be. Buying life, auto, and property insurance products involves something uncertain in exchange for a premium. That is, you don't know if you'll have a car accident. Thus, chance is involved. Some forms of insurance, like groups coming together to self-insure, are permissible. However, publicly traded insurance companies don't sell this type of insurance product.

Another investing principle of halal is to avoid haram (forbidden) businesses or industries. This prohibition is like the tenets of many other socially responsible investing principles. Investors can't own companies that derive substantial income, defined as more than 5% of their total income, from processing or selling alcohol, tobacco, pork, and weapons, or from engaging in gambling and pornography. One deviation from common sustainable investment principles is the type of stock ownership that is permissible. Common stock is acceptable, but preferred stock is not. Preferred stock usually pays a constant dividend and is often considered more of a fixed-income security than equity. Islamic finance treats preferred stock more like a bond than a stock.

> " . . . our job is to encourage clients to handle wealth for God's purpose."
> —Erik Daniels

Halal investing recognizes the impossibility of being 100% compliant with Shariah. You may buy stock in compliance, but then the company's business model may change by acquiring too much debt or starting a prohibited new business line. Halal investors have a procedure for reacting to this problem called a *purification process*. This process estimates the profit derived from the noncompliance that the investor can donate to a charity. This calculation often involves corporate profits derived from small portions (defined by AAOIFI guidelines) of interest revenue.

The prohibition on hoarding gold and silver stems from the idea that hoarding a scarce resource lowers the standard of living for those who cannot obtain that resource. This notion was especially true when gold and silver were the primary media of exchange for commerce. Therefore, owning gold and silver to buy goods and services is allowed. However, investing in gold and silver crosses the line into hoarding money and is thus prohibited.

Finally, responsible investing for Muslims goes beyond avoiding the products and services that cause harm to society. It also means helping those in need. Muslims often accomplish this through Zakat, the annual sharing of wealth. Zakat is a

Muslim obligation for those who meet the wealth criteria to donate a specific portion of their wealth to charitable causes each year.

How can investors consider Jewish faith-based values?

A fundamental principle of the Jewish social and economic system is the divine origins of wealth. Judaism acknowledges pursuing wealth if it happens in a manner that also contributes to the collective welfare and under the sanctity of Jewish law. It's a person's responsibility to grow and protect individual and communal resources. According to this view, people are merely temporary stewards of wealth, allowing them to direct the wealth toward religious and communal ends. An example is the principle of *shmitah*, which is the practice of forgiving all debts. Therefore, Judaism requires that a person act as both an economic agent and as a moral agent. The Jewish values that guide investing encourage gains for both the individual and the community.

Jewish faith-based investing revolves around the values of *tikkun olam* (repair of the world) and *tzedek* (justice). For modern Jewish investors, repairing the world suggests aligning investments to combat climate change as a call to address one of today's most pressing global challenges. Thus, Jewish investors may exclude the worst polluting companies or seek innovative companies at the forefront of a low-carbon economy transition.

Interpreting the value of justice could occur in several ways. For example, one Jewish investor might consider justice to mean the importance of gender diversity and equality. Thus, investors can use some social criteria in ESG data to identify companies with good gender equality and social practices. On the other hand, another Jewish investor may see justice as applying to human rights conditions. Thus, this sustainable investor would exclude firms with records of treating their workers poorly or have supply chains with such reputations.

Lastly, many Jewish people around the world feel a strong connection to Israel. Support for Israel is a core value that Jewish investors can incorporate. They do this by investing in companies headquartered in Israel or doing business in Israel. This action is the opposite of the old South African boycott. The boycott of South Africa intended to starve the economy of capital, thereby forcing the government to abandon its apartheid system. By providing their capital to Israeli firms, Jewish investors contribute to the collective welfare of the Jewish state.

How might socially progressive values affect investment choice?

The SRI movement may have its roots in religious values, but its progressive ideals have become prominent. For example, the basis for one's attitudes against tobacco is often health concerns, not moral concerns. Similarly, attitudes against alcohol use stem from health concerns and community safety. The opposition to gambling also comes from its impact on communities. Thus, political ideologies, not religious ones, are what drive these social attitudes. Moreover, common SRI concerns, like the environment, labor practices, and social justice, appeal more to socially progressive people than religious ones. Indeed, some progressive values, like supporting firms that provide health benefits to employees' gay and lesbian partners, directly conflict with some religious values.

Social progressives view economics through the lens of social justice. Thus, they support education equality, women's health resources, criminal justice reform, universal health care, workplace equality, a high minimum wage, and labor unions. However, these initiatives cost taxpayers money and require regulation. Thus, they seek higher taxes on the wealthy but distrust Wall Street. In many ways, this view is the opposite of politically conservative values that promote low

"Business can be a source of progressive change."
—Jerry Greenfield

taxes, smaller government, and the power of free markets. Not surprisingly, these socially progressive political ideologies identify with the Democratic Party in the United States.

Democrats and Republicans not only have different political ideologies, but they also invest differently. Consider a mutual fund manager who makes personal political contributions to the Democratic Party. Another fund manager contributes to the Republican Party. By examining these mutual fund portfolio stock allocations, researchers can tell how Democrats invest compared to Republicans. An analysis of thousands of mutual fund holdings shows that those fund managers who donate to the Democratic Party own fewer socially irresponsible firms, such as tobacco, firearms, defense, and natural resources industries, than Republican Party donor fund managers. Political contributors tend to own companies' stock managed by chief executive officers (CEOs) with the same political leanings. These political leanings reflect individual fund manager preferences that are tangential to the fund's stated investment goals. No investor resources on Democrat or Republican value-based investing are available. Yet, many publications are available on what investors should own when a particular political party controls the government.

What is patriotic investing?

In a time of national crisis, citizens often feel compelled to do their patriotic duty, including their investment choices. For example, consider the patriotic promotion of U.S. war bonds like the Civil War Soldier Bonds of 1865 and the post-Pearl Harbor Liberty Bonds of 1945. After the terrorist attacks on September 11, 2001, the government renamed Treasury Bonds (Series I and EE.) Patriot Bonds. Sales of Series I and EE bonds rose 43% over the next year.

To many people, patriotic investing is more than just a rallying cry during a time of crisis. It's

"I think patriotism is like charity—it begins at home."
—Henry James

a long-term philosophy of supporting fellow citizens. Over the past decade, a powerful movement to "buy local" emerged. Local businesses are our neighbors. They hire local workers and make their purchases locally. Local businesses also support local nonprofits, events, and teams. Thus, buying local promotes sustainability for a community. Over the years, politicians in many countries have made similar appeals for their citizens to support their countries' businesses and workers. In the United States, former Presidents Woodrow Wilson, Warren G. Harding, and Donald Trump used the slogan "America First," and Senator Elizabeth Warren offered "A Plan for Economic Patriotism." Although many consumers choose products based on price and quality, some consumers prefer domestically produced goods. They often prefer domestic investments too. Thus, a patriotic portfolio that supports fellow citizens consists of domestic companies' stocks and bonds producing or manufacturing products at home.

However, some investors take patriotic investing even further. They invest in securities that they deem essential to supporting and defending the country. These investments might include local and national government bonds, weapons manufacturers, and defense contractors.

One problem that patriotic investors may face is reduced diversification opportunities. The preference for local investing causes investors to concentrate their stock holdings at home. This notion refers to a *home bias*. Well-diversified portfolios tend to include international investments.

How are stocks found using negative and positive social screens?

Once you understand which values you want to incorporate into your investing, you need to find stocks that meet your criteria. You may find that you can sort companies into three groups: (1) those with stocks sharing the same value, (2) those violating that value, and (3) those with stock indifferent or unrelated to the value. For example, consider a personal value to invest in a climate-sustainable manner. Oil-producing firms like ExxonMobil violate this principle. On the other hand, green energy firms like SunPower Corp, as well as many companies not producing or using fossil fuels, like Microsoft, are consistent with that value. One method of grouping stocks for each strategy involves negative and positive screening techniques. Negative screens identify the companies and industries you want to avoid, while positive screens identify the companies that embody the values you hold.

The most common types of negative screens prohibit certain products. These screens can completely exclude the stocks of companies that produce or sell the product. The most common products and activities restricted from the portfolio are alcohol, tobacco, gambling, defense/weapons, nuclear energy, pornography, or contraceptives. Other negative screening techniques allow some revenue from these products but limit the percentage of overall revenues derived from those products. For example, investors may view a hotel and resort company as a purveyor of these restricted products. However, it might offer customers premium television channels that include pornography. If the hotel firm derives 0.1% of its revenue from those channel premiums, is that enough to eliminate it as an investment choice? If the hotel firm owns one hotel-casino in Nevada that contributes 1% of the firm's total revenue, should investors eliminate it as an investment choice? If an investor wants to exclude tobacco or alcohol from the portfolio, avoiding Philip Morris, Imperial Brands, Boston Beer, and Willamette Valley Vineyards seems obvious. Yet, some grocery stores and gas stations sell cigarettes and alcohol. Many restaurants also sell alcohol. Does the investor want to avoid all the firms in these industries too? The answers reflect investors' personal choices. However, taking a more restrictive approach results in eliminating more companies.

> "Sustainability is no longer about doing less harm. It's about doing more good."
> —Jochen Zeitz

For many values-based investors, avoiding offensive companies is insufficient. Investing in companies in a group whose operations are indifferent to the value is not particularly interesting. Consequently, investors seek out companies in the group that share their values. They accomplish this objective through positive screens that identify the firms with desirable environmental, social, and governance (ESG) characteristics. These firms are less likely to experience high-impact negative news about environmental or social issues, like BP's *Deepwater Horizon* oil spill in the Gulf of Mexico. One concern about exclusively using positive screens to form a portfolio is that the number of stocks that pass positive screens tends to be small and concentrated in a few industries. Thus, the portfolio may lack diversification and so will hold more risk than desired.

Sustainable investors and SRI mutual funds can use negative and positive screens to form a values-based and well-diversified portfolio. For example, a negative screen is easy to implement and effectively avoids certain problematic products like tobacco and alcohol. However, investors may need to use a positive screen technique to identify the firms with socially desirable values like having women on the board of directors or supporting specific social justice issues.

Implementing positive or negative screens is not as simple as it may sound. Although many free online stock screeners are available, most are not sophisticated enough to execute an SRI filter search. For example, most screeners are good at filtering firms by size, P/E ratio, dividend, industry, and stock index. However, they can't exclude industries and specific products or identify firms with desirable social characteristics. For more sophisticated screening programs, you need to look to the tools offered by your stock brokerage firm and subscription-based services.

What stock indices benchmark socially responsible firms?

One method for finding socially responsible stocks is to examine the components in socially responsible stock indices. Those stocks have been "cleared" using sustainable screens. Thus, if your values are consistent with the index methodology's values, you can let the index do some of the work for you. Socially responsible stock indices are available from index firms like Dow Jones and independent sources focused on sustainability.

- *MSCI KLD 400 Social Index.* The first socially responsible investing index, the Domini 400 Social Index, launched in 1990. The index is now called the MSCI KLD 400 Social Index. It excludes companies associated with alcohol, tobacco, gambling, civilian firearms, military weapons, nuclear power, adult entertainment, and genetically modified organisms. In addition, it includes the best ESG rated firms in each sector, a best-in-class approach. The index consists of 400 small-, mid-, and large-capitalization (cap) U.S. companies.
- *Humankind U.S. Equity Index.* Humankind Investments LLC sponsors this index. It includes the common stocks of U.S. companies determined to positively impact humanity, defined as investors, customers, employees, and society members. The index contains 1,000 stocks.
- *S&P Dow Jones Indices.* This source has many SRI indices. For example, Dow Jones has a family of nine sustainability indices that comprise country, regional, and global benchmarks. The S&P ESG Index family is made up of 23 indices launched in 2019 that group stocks by country, region, and often by capitalization (small-, mid-, large-cap). These indices focus on firms that integrate ESG factors into their core activities while staying close to the S&P broad market indices they

"Sustainability makes good business sense, and we're all on the same team at the end of the day. That's the truth about the human condition."

—Paul Polman

mimic. For example, the S&P 500 ESG Index has an association with the S&P 500 Index.

- *MSCI index*. MSCI is a popular purveyor of stock and bond indices. Besides the previously mentioned MSCI KLD 400 Social Index, dozens of other MSCI SRI indices are available. The ESG Leaders indices group encompasses 12 indices that target the highest ESG-rated performance in various markets worldwide. The MSCI SRI Indexes use a best-in-class approach. The *best-in-class approach* to sustainable investing means investing in companies that are leaders in their sector to meet ESG criteria. Their MSCI ESG Rating first ranks companies within each sector. Stocks in the top 25% are eligible for inclusion in the index. Another important index is the MSCI ACWI Sustainable Impact Index. This index identifies firms aligned with the Sustainable Development Goals (SDGs) of the UN. These SDGs consist of five actionable themes: (1) basic needs, (2) empowerment, (3) climate change, (4) natural capital, and (5) governance.

- *Bloomberg*. Bloomberg has several socially responsible indices. It focuses on providing SRI benchmarks for institutional investors. Bloomberg's strategy covers the U.S. large-cap space and the value, growth, and dividend yield arenas.

  o *Bloomberg SASB US Large Cap ESG Index*. This index is a socially responsible equity benchmark that chooses from the largest 500 companies to optimize exposure to their proprietary R-Factor™. This factor measures a company's performance related to financially material ESG challenges. Although the number of firms in the index can fluctuate, it hovers around 150 companies.

  o *Bloomberg SASB US Large Cap ESG Ex-Controversies Index*. Bloomberg follows a similar process to identify firms in the Bloomberg SASB US Large Cap ESG Ex-Controversies Index. This index is R-Factor optimized after excluding companies with an extreme ESG event or business lines, including weapons and firearms, United Nations Global Compact violations, coal extraction, or tobacco.

o *Other Bloomberg indices.* Bloomberg also offers the Bloomberg SASB US Growth ESG Ex-Controversies Index, the Bloomberg SASB US Value ESG Ex-Controversies Index, and the Bloomberg SASB US Dividend Yield ESG Ex-Controversies Index.

Due to the rising popularity of sustainable investing, the number of socially responsible indices has skyrocketed. Thus, you should be able to find one or more indices that reflect your value.

What are Morningstar's Sustainability Scores?

To assist investors, Morningstar (at Morningstar.com) has an ESG rating system to evaluate how effectively each mutual fund invests in a sustainable portfolio, the Morningstar Sustainability Score.

Morningstar's Sustainability Score begins with Sustainalytics' company-level ESG Risk Rating, which measures the degree to which a company's economic value may be at risk due to ESG factors (i.e., unmanaged residual ESG risk). The score represents unmanaged ESG risk, with lower values representing less unmanaged risk. The Sustainability Score is the sum of the individual E, S, and G scores. Besides the Sustainability Score and individual ESG ratings provided for each company, Morningstar sorts the Score into five risk categories: Negligible, Low, Medium, High, and Severe. You can find these scores for each company at https://www.sustain alytics.com/esg-ratings. For example, the ESG Risk Ratings in early 2021 of several well-known companies are:

- Apple Inc., 16.7 (Low Risk)
- Tesla Inc., 31.3 (High Risk)

- General Electric, 42.6 (Severe Risk)
- Bank of America, 26.3 (Medium Risk)
- Meta, 31.6 (High Risk)
- Amazon.com, 27.4 (Medium Risk)
- Intel Corp., 16.9 (Low Risk)
- Pfizer Inc., 25.3 (Medium Risk)
- Walmart Inc., 27.5 (Medium Risk)
- Beyond Meat, Inc., 43.5 (Severe Risk)

Are some of these ESG Risk Ratings surprising? For example, a company may do well in one ESG area like pollution but do poorly in another, like human rights in their supply chain. Table 3.1 shows the 20 material ESG issues that were examined.

Morningstar uses this company-level measure and calculates an asset-weighted average ESG risk score for each mutual fund portfolio. A higher portfolio sustainability or ESG risk score represents a worse ESG risk profile. Conversely, a lower sustainability risk score indicates that the mutual fund has a more ESG friendly portfolio.

Only two of the 20 material ESG issues relate directly to climate change and greenhouse gas measurements. Thus, a

Table 3.1 Sustainalytics' 20 Material ESG Issues

ESG Issue Categories	
Environmental and social impact of products and services	Human capital
Business ethics	Human rights
Data privacy and security	Human rights–Supply chain
Bribery and corruption	Access to basic services
Community relations	Emissions, effluents, and waste
Land use and biodiversity	Carbon–Products and services
Land use and biodiversity–Supply chain	Carbon–Own operations
Occupational health and safety	ESG Integration–financials
Product governance	Resource use
Resilience	Resource use–Supply chain

company could score poorly in carbon emissions but well on the other 18 material issues, resulting in a moderate sustainability risk category.

What are Morningstar's Carbon Risk Scores?

To focus more directly on climate change, Morningstar began reporting fund-level carbon risk in May 2018. Again, Morningstar starts with a Sustainalytics' company-level measure, the Carbon Risk Ratings. A company's carbon risk shows the degree of alignment between a firm's activities and products and the transition to a low-carbon economy. It goes beyond just a carbon footprint to a direct assessment of material carbon risk.

The score assesses two dimensions: exposure and management. Exposure measures the degree to which carbon risks are material across the firm's entire value chain, including its supply chain, own operation, and products and services. Management measures a firm's ability to manage and the quality of the management approach, reducing emissions and related carbon risks. The Carbon Risk Score measures a company's remaining unmanaged carbon risk after considering its efforts to mitigate carbon risk through its management activities. Morningstar's Carbon Risk Score is the asset-weighted sum of the Sustainalytics Carbon Risk Scores of its holdings. Thus, higher Carbon Risk Scores denote higher carbon risks in the fund's portfolio.

Investors can check Morningstar's Sustainability Score and the Morningstar Carbon Risk Score to evaluate how well a mutual fund performs on the ESG and carbon risk dimensions. To understand what these measurements are like, consider the Fidelity 500 Index fund. This fund replicates the S&P 500 Index. Thus, it represents a proxy for the overall U.S. stock market. In early 2021, this index fund had a Sustainability Rating of 22.06 and a Carbon Risk Score of 6.24. Table 3.2 shows the ratings for some popular U.S. mutual funds.

Table 3.2 Morningstar Social Responsibility Ratings for Popular U.S. Mutual Funds

Mutual Fund	Sustainability				Carbon Risk
	Total	E	S	G	
Fidelity 500 Index Fund	22.06	3.75	10.45	7.87	6.24
Fidelity Contrafund	21.64	2.49	10.34	8.34	3.64
American Funds Growth Fund of America	23.55	3.26	11.23	8.10	5.25
American Funds Fundamental Investors Fund	23.39	4.64	10.50	7.67	6.40
Dodge & Cox International Stock	25.04	4.91	10.61	9.53	10.61
T. Rowe Price Blue Chip Growth	21.50	2.03	11.06	8.36	2.09
Harbor Capital Appreciation	20.97	1.96	10.66	8.05	2.48
JPMorgan Mid Cap Value	23.24	6.49	9.30	7.36	14.79

Let's compare each fund with the Fidelity 500 Index Fund. For example, the Fidelity Contrafund has a Sustainability Score that is slightly less than the market overall. However, this comes from a lower E (environmental) rating that overcomes the higher G (governance) rating. Confirmation of the lower environmentally friendly rating comes from the Carbon Risk Score, which is much lower than the overall market. Several other observations are meaningful. First, the Dodge & Cox International Stock fund has the highest Sustainability Score and Carbon Risk Score for its portfolio. This result is likely because it focuses on owning non-U.S. companies and many countries have less stringent socially responsible laws and enforcement. Second, the T. Rowe Price Blue Chip Growth and Harbor Capital Appreciation funds have lower sustainability and carbon risk portfolios. Although these are popular funds, they don't purport to be socially responsible.

Where can investors find socially responsible mutual funds?

Many mutual funds offer investors socially responsible portfolios. As discussed earlier, your values may differ from those of other investors. The overall demand for SRI funds is significant, and the objectives sought vary. Thus, you can choose among many funds. You must sort through their investment objectives to determine which funds match your values. Morningstar lists over 700 mutual funds available that mention sustainable principles in their prospectus. Many ETFs are also available.

Several mutual fund families use ESG principles in all their funds. For example, consider these popular socially oriented mutual funds families:

- *Calvert*. Calvert claims to have launched the first fund to integrate ESG factors with traditional financial metrics in 1982. It now has 27 funds incorporating ESG factors and covering stocks, bonds, and international markets.
- *Pax World*. Pax World offers 11 different sustainable funds and claims to have launched the first U.S. fund to integrate social and financial criteria in 1971.
- *Domini Impact Investments*. This fund family began its first fund in 1991. Its funds focus on incorporating Universal Human Dignity and Ecological Sustainability goals. The fund family offers five funds focusing on these goals.
- *Parnassus Investments*. Parnassus Investments has five funds that are fossil fuel–free and fully integrate ESG and fundamental analysis. The first fund in this family started in 1992.
- *Green Century*. Green Century invests in environmental innovators and sustainable companies. This fund family seeks firms involved in energy efficiency, renewable energy, and sustainable agriculture.

Sustainable investing has become commonplace. So no wonder many sizeable mutual fund families now offer ESG portfolios, like BlackRock, Boston, DWS, Eventide, Fidelity, Goldman Sachs, Hartford, Invesco, Janus, JPMorgan, PIMCO, TIAA-CREF, and Vanguard. You may already own a fund offered by one or more of these financial firms. If so, investigating their specific ESG offerings and reallocating your investment to them is simple if they meet your value-based standards. Some funds target specific objectives. For example, Fidelity offers funds specializing in ESG themes like water, the environment, and women's leadership. Some funds use negative screens to exclude firms of specific products, while other funds focus on tilting the portfolio toward firms with positive ESG characteristics. Other funds use a best-in-class approach.

Table 3.3 shows several ESG mutual funds with their Sustainability Ratings and Carbon Risk Scores from Morningstar. However, you can choose among hundreds of ESG-oriented mutual funds and ETFs. The first row is the Fidelity 500 Index Fund from Table 3.2, a proxy for the overall market. All the funds listed have a lower (better) Sustainability Rating than the overall market. In addition, all but one fund has a portfolio with a lower carbon risk than the market. You

Table 3.3 Morningstar Social Responsibility Ratings for Sustainable Mutual Funds

Mutual Fund	Sustainability				Carbon Risk
	Total	E	S	G	
Fidelity 500 Index Fund	22.06	3.75	10.45	7.87	6.24
Calvert Equity Fund	19.00	2.80	9.18	7.02	4.58
Pax ESG Beta Quality Fund	19.77	2.88	9.54	7.35	4.91
Domini Impact Equity Fund	20.56	2.65	9.31	7.53	4.02
Parnassus Core Equity Fund	20.08	3.66	9.59	6.83	4.86
Green Century Equity Fund	19.97	2.88	9.66	7.23	4.43
BlackRock Advantage ESG US Equity Fund	20.13	2.91	9.50	7.25	5.44
DWS ESG Core Equity Fund	20.83	3.14	9.59	7.38	5.50
Hartford Climate Opportunities Fund	21.60	5.71	7.63	6.26	8.30
Goldman Sachs US Equity ESG Fund	20.50	3.36	9.34	7.22	4.44
TIAA-CREF Social Choice Equity Fund	20.82	3.31	9.11	6.83	6.09

can also compare these sustainable funds with the traditional funds shown in Table 3.2.

What exchange-traded funds have socially responsible portfolios?

An *exchange-traded fund* (ETF) is a security tracking a particular set of equities. It trades on a stock exchange just like a regular stock. Each ETF has a ticker symbol to identify it for easy trading through any stock brokerage account. Most ETFs are indexed to track a market, sector, commodity, or another asset. Thus, most ETFs try to replicate the index performance. As discussed earlier, many socially responsible indices are available. Not surprisingly, many socially responsible stock ETFs are available to track those indices. ESG-oriented ETFs cover the U.S. market, the Europe, Australasia, and Far East (EAFE) market, and emerging markets. Here are several examples:

- Fidelity US Sustainability Index ETF (ticker: FITLX)
- Goldman Sachs Just US Lg Cap Eq ETF (ticker: JUST)
- Humankind ETF (ticker: HKND)
- IQ Candriam ESG US Equity ETF (ticker: IQSU)
- iShares ESG Screened S&P Mid-Cap ETF (ticker: XJH)
- iShares ESG Screened S&P Small-Cap ETF (ticker: XJR)
- iShares ESG Aware MSCI EAFE ETF (ticker: ESGD)
- iShares ESG Aware MSCI EM ETF (ticker: ESGE)
- iShares ESG Advanced MSCI USA ETF (ticker: USXF)
- iShares ESG Advanced MSCI EM ETF (ticker: EMXF)
- JPMorgan Carbon Transition US Eq ETF (ticker: JCTR)
- SPDR MSCI EAFE Fossil Fuel Free ETF (ticker: EFAX)
- SPDR MSCI ACWI Low Carbon Target ETF (ticker: LOWC)
- Vanguard ESG International Stock ETF (ticker: VSGX)
- Vanguard FTSE Social Index ETF (ticker: VFTNX)
- Xtrackers MSCI USA ESG Leaders Eq ETF (ticker: USSG)

You can further explore the ESG ratings for ETFs through Morningstar's Sustainability and Carbon Risk Scores.

Where can investors find sustainable bonds and other fixed-income funds?

The SRI movement began with an equity focus. That is, socially conscious investors focused on buying the stock of companies that aligned with their values. However, ESG scores generally apply to companies themselves. Thus, all securities issued by a company are assigned the same ESG characteristics, regardless of whether they are stocks or bonds. Therefore, investors who want to buy corporate bonds consistent with their social values can obtain ESG characteristics by examining a firm's stock. For example, many sustainable investors would avoid owning Philip Morris's stock because it manufactures tobacco products. Likewise, bond investors would avoid Philip Morris corporate bonds, too.

Savvy investors know that well-diversified portfolios include bonds. Sustainable investors can invest in bond portfolios through mutual funds and ETFs. Like equity funds, ESG bond funds can orient themselves toward different values by emphasizing one ESG aspect more than the others. The main types of bonds differ based on who issues them, such as government bonds, corporate bonds, and municipal bonds. Another way to delineate bonds is by time to maturity (short, medium, and long term) and default risk, which is the risk of the lender not repaying the debt obligation. ESG mutual funds and ETFs are available for all different bond classes.

Here are some examples of ESG bond mutual funds:

- Calvert Green Bond Fund
- Domini Impact Bond Fund
- JPMorgan Sustainable Municipal Income Fund
- Pax High Yield Bond Fund
- PIMCO Climate Bond Fund
- Vanguard ESG US Corporate Bond Fund
- TIAA-CREF Core Impact Bond Fund

Here are some examples of ESG Bond ETFs:

- Fidelity Sustainability Bond ETF (ticker: FNDSX)
- iShares ESG Aware USD Corporate Bond ETF (ticker: SUSC)
- iShares ESG Aware 1–5 Year USD Corporate Bond ETF (ticker: SUSB)
- iShares ESG Advanced Total USD Bond Market ETF (ticker: USB)
- NuShares ESG US Aggregate Bond ETF (ticker: NUBD)
- Nuveen ESG High Yield Corporate Bond ETF (ticker: NUHY)
- Sage ESG Intermediate Credit ETF (ticker: GUDB)

Balanced and target funds with an ESG focus are also available.

- Green Century Balanced Fund
- Natixis Sustainable Future 2040 Fund
- Parnassus Fixed Income Fund

What online resources are available for researching a values-based investment approach?

Here are some websites that provide information about values-based investing.

- The Paris Climate Agreement offers recommendations on converting the economy to become more sustainable: https://unfccc.int/process-and-meetings/the-paris-agreement/the-paris-agreement
- Socially Responsible Investment Guidelines for the United States Conference of Catholic Bishops offer Catholics and other Christians policies and standards for faith-based investing: https://www.usccb.org/about/financial-reporting/socially-responsible-investment-guidelines

- This description of the S&P 500 Catholic Values ETF allows investors to identify a list of acceptable stocks consistent with the Catholic faith: https://www.globalxetfs.com/funds/cath
- American Baptist Home Mission Society revised its "Guidelines Relating to Social Criteria for Investments" to promote a global community built on justice and sustainability: https://abhms.org/ministries/healing-communities/socially-responsible-investment
- Accounting and Auditing Organization for Islamic Financial Institutions publishes principles for finance and investing practices in accordance with Shariah: https://aaoifi.com/?lang=en
- Sustainalytics ESG Risk Ratings produces company-level ratings for the environment, social, and governance aspects individually and a combined rating: https://www.sustainalytics.com/esg-ratings
- Morningstar shows Sustainability Scores and Carbon Risk Scores for each mutual fund and ETF: https://www.morningstar.com

Takeaways

Social, political, and religious beliefs are the basis for most values-based investing. The key is to understand your values and the strength of your convictions. Then you can find investment opportunities that build portfolios that align with your beliefs. Here are some essential lessons from this chapter.

- Determine your set of social values and the strength of those convictions.
- Understand the community and employee values that matter to you.
- Assess the human and civil rights policies of a company, including its supply chain.

- Seek firms whose products and operations are consistent with fighting climate change.
- Evaluate how your religious beliefs, if any, should direct your investment values.
- Gauge how your political values should affect your investment choices.
- Ascertain how your patriotism influences your investment values.
- Pursue positive social aspect companies along with avoiding harmful product companies.
- Identify socially responsible stock indices that share the same values as you do.
- Review Morningstar's Sustainability Scores and Carbon Risk Scores for your investment opportunities.
- Identify mutual funds and ETFs that align with your values.

4

SUSTAINABLE INVESTING

MAKING MONEY WHILE DOING GOOD

> Society is demanding that companies, both public and private, serve a social purpose. Therefore, to prosper over time, every company must not only deliver financial performance but also show how it makes a positive contribution to society.
>
> —Larry Fink, CEO of Blackrock

Deciding how to invest money, either for yourself or for others, can be complicated. For traditional investing, the primary criterion is profitability. If you're interested in sustainable investing, the process becomes even more challenging because you're adding another layer of complexity. The motivation for sustainable investing differs among investors. However, their concern with integrating personal values and societal issues into investment decision making indicates that they're looking for more than just a monetary return.

> Making money while doing good is intuitively appealing because it has the potential to combine the best of two worlds that were frequently considered opposites.
>
> —Cornelia Caseau and Giles Grolleau

Although once a niche investment approach, sustainable investing is becoming the new normal for many investors. For example, many investors are no longer satisfied with just making money. These investors increasingly want products and solutions across asset classes tailored to their interests and values. They're not just looking at such investments for their feel-good characteristics and ability to promote sustainable development and business practices. They also want to improve their investments' risk/return profile and attain more effective portfolio diversification.

> "The business of business should not be about money. It should be about responsibility. It should be about public good, not private greed."
> —Anita Roddick

As sustainable investing has grown and evolved, so has the level of sophistication of this investment space. It can be challenging because investors have different motivations or objectives and face different approaches to sustainable investing. As a result, there's neither a "one size fits all" approach nor a standard classification system for ESG strategies. Instead, these investors have many methods to help them meet their goals. For example, SRI-Connect identifies 21 distinct strategies (https://www.sri-connect.com/index.php). This chapter helps sort through investment approaches and choices that provide more than just a financial return.

How does traditional investing differ from sustainable investing?

Think about investors consisting of a spectrum of different types. At one end of the continuum, traditional investors pursue profit and shareholder returns above all other considerations regardless of an investment's impact on society. Thus, making money is their only concern; they're willing to invest in anything if the risk-return trade-off

> "There is one and only one responsibility of business: to use its resources and engage in activities designed to increase its profits so long as it stays within the rules of the game."
> —Milton Friedman

is sufficiently attractive. At the other end of the spectrum are impact investors who want to generate positive, measurable social and environmental impact in addition to conventional financial returns.

> "Companies should not have a singular view of profitability. There needs to be a balance between commerce and social responsibility."
>
> —Howard Schultz

Savvy investors certainly want to earn a return on their investments, but what if the company makes money by doing "bad" or objectionable things such as offering harmful products, polluting the environment, or exploiting its workers or community? Such companies aren't socially responsible. Is that the way you want to earn a return? For many investors, the answer is no. They want their investments to have both a financial and extra-financial dimension. Such investors are picky about how the industries and companies in which they invest make money. They want to grow their money while doing good. Some want to invest in social causes meaningful to them. Consequently, they make investments that reflect their values and beliefs.

What are the potential concerns about sustainable investing?

Sustainable investing isn't without drawbacks. Here are a few.

- *A reduced opportunity set of investments.* A frequently voiced concern is limiting your investment options by excluding many investments with attractive return characteristics.

Your investment pool shrinks when you filter out investments based on various environmental, social, and governance (ESG) or other criteria, which in turn reduces your ability to diversify your portfolio.

> "Companies with their eye on their 'triple-bottom-line' outperform their less fastidious peers on the stock market."
>
> —*The Economist*

Some excluded companies may have low ESG scores but offer quality products and services accompanied by outstanding returns. Thus, you may fear that filtering out these investment opportunities leaves some great investment returns on the table. This situation is a type of *constrained optimization* in which you optimize an objective function for some variables in the presence of constraints on those variables. Some believe that sustainable investments generally underperform conventional ones. Not surprisingly, empirical evidence on this subject is mixed. Recent research suggests that sustainable strategies perform similarly or better than traditional methods. Thus, you may not have to sacrifice financial returns when making sustainable investments. However, keep in mind that sustainable investors have dual objectives: making money and doing good. They're concerned with profitability and want their investments to have a nonfinancial impact aligned with their values.

- *A chance of fraud, deception, and hype.* Interest in sustainable investing is so great that it has attracted financial fraudsters, ethically challenged salespeople, and those prone to hype developing trends. These nefarious operators prey on less knowledgeable investors who are emotionally devoted to making the world better. If you aren't cautious, you can become a victim of an individual acting in disreputable, unethical, or unscrupulous ways.

    Investors should be cautious of a financial firm publishing research supposedly showing that a particular socially responsible product has superior returns because the study could be biased to "push" an investment vehicle. Instead, you're probably better off relying on sound academic research, which is often more rigorous and objective.
- *A marketing ploy.* A third danger is that some companies and funds project the image of being socially responsible as merely a marketing strategy. For example, they put a "green" or "ESG" label on an existing investment without any real commitment to being socially responsible. This behavior is called *greenwashing*, a deceptive practice of

conveying a false impression or providing misleading information about how a company's products are environmentally friendly. Thus, proving that a company is considering ESG factors can be difficult.

If you're investing in a mutual fund, you should ensure that it's voting on shareholder resolutions relating to ESG issues. In colloquial terms, you don't just want a company to "talk the talk" but also to "walk the walk." Be cautious because some businesses employ this marketing ploy. You should follow the principle of *caveat emptor* or buyer beware. If you're making the investment decision, you alone are responsible for checking the investment's suitability before buying it. You need to look behind the corporate veil and discover if the company or fund is truthful. A creative marketing campaign can make perception appear like reality.

> "It takes 20 years to build a reputation and five minutes to ruin it. If you think about that, you'll do things differently."
>
> —Warren Buffett

For example, Volkswagen (VW) portrayed itself as an environmentally conscious business by promoting clean diesel cars. However, as noted in Chapter 2, the Volkswagen Group installed "defeat devices" in 11 million diesel-powered vehicles worldwide to cheat emissions tests. This scandal, which came to be known as "Dieselgate" or "Emissionsgate" started in September 2015, when the U.S. Environmental Protection Agency (EPA) issued a notice of violation of the Clean Air Act to the German automaker. The consequences of the company's actions were dire, resulting in a massive decline in its stock price immediately after the news announcement and the eventual resignation or suspension of several high-ranking executives. As of June 1, 2020, the scandal had cost VW $33.3 billion in fines, penalties, financial settlements, and buyback costs.

- *Different meanings of sustainable investing.* Another draw-back is that sustainable investing means various things to people. It's highly ambiguous and subjective—one size doesn't fit all. It can be challenging to define and measure objectively. Thus, if you're selecting a socially conscious mutual fund or exchange-traded fund (ETF), you need to know the criteria its fund managers use to implement the fund's strategy of selecting securities for its portfolio. In other words, different funds use different approaches and standards. No single criterion exists for defining such investments. Therefore, make sure that how a company or fund views sustainable investing is consistent with your views.
- *Higher potential costs.* Another potential pitfall is that fees associated with investing in socially responsible and sustainable mutual funds can be higher than regular funds. Portfolio managers need to be vigilant that such funds remain socially conscious. Higher fees can be a drag on performance. Thus, there's a cost for doing good if you're not careful.
- *The difficulty of measuring impact.* Quantifying the effect of investing beyond financial returns can be difficult, especially in the short run. Although various sources such as MSCI, S&P Global, and Refinitiv/S-Network publish ESG ratings and indices, they're unavailable for some investment categories. You also need to be aware of the construction of such ratings and indices. In short, determining whether you're making a difference in the world can be complicated. As a result, you may "feel" better but may lack an objective basis for justifying those feelings.

What is the screening approach to sustainable investing?

Figure 4.1 shows that screening can take several forms.

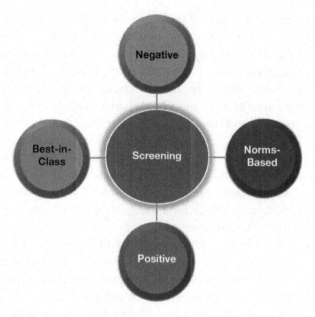

Figure 4.1 Types of Screening Approaches

- *Negative/exclusionary screening.* With negative screening, investors apply a nonfinancial screen to a universe of investment alternatives to identify candidates. Thus, this approach deliberately excludes specific industries, business activities, or products from an investment portfolio based on ethics, values, or principles. For example, some investors may avoid fossil fuel stocks for being detrimental to a sustainable economy. They view these companies as engaging in undesirable or controversial activities, so they don't want their money invested in such activities.

Although negative screening is one of the earliest tools used by socially responsible investors to build value-aligned portfolios, it's the most common sustainable

"Sustainability is no longer about doing less harm. It's about doing more good."
—Jochen Zeitz

investment strategy globally in terms of asset values. Over time, however, other approaches have gained popularity. For example, some negative screens involve weapons, tobacco, gambling, alcohol, fossil fuels, nuclear power, adult entertainment, human rights abuses, environment/climate, genetically modified organisms, and animal welfare. Investors can also use negative screens to enact political and social changes. For instance, investors used an early form of negative screening called divestment to fight against the apartheid regime in South Africa in the 1980s. *Divestment* is the process of selling an asset, such as stock, to satisfy some financial, social, or political goals. Negative screens generally result in more "black-and-white" types of decisions. However, such an approach may involve opportunity costs by barring prominent stocks from portfolios.

- *Norms-based screening.* Norms-based screening, a subcategory of negative screening, sorts investments based on compliance with relevant international norms and standards such as the UN Global Compact, the Kyoto Protocol, and the UN Declaration of Human Rights. It excludes investments that don't comply with the norms or adjusts their weighting according to their degree of compliance.

- *Positive screening.* An alternative to negative screening is *positive screening,* which involves selecting companies based on positive characteristics. Unlike negative screening, positive screens often require analyzing complex issues affecting the community, diversity, labor relations, environment, and product quality and safety. In a sense, positive and negative screens are two sides of the same coin. However, positive screening can tilt the selection in several directions.

- The *best-in-class approach* is a comparative investment style that involves investing in companies leading the universe or sector to meet ESG criteria. Thus, investors select better-positioned companies for the future and avoid those likely to underperform or fail. Therefore, it takes a holistic view of companies' commitment to sustainability by considering macro- and micro-economic factors. The underlying logic of this "invest in the best and avoid the rest" strategy makes this pragmatic approach a relatively safe bet. It also creates the right incentives by encouraging managers to improve ESG performance in an integrated way to promote positive changes.

o The *financially weighted best-in-class* approach, a variant of best-in-class, incorporates financial and ESG factors into the best-in-class decision-making process but gives additional weight to the sustainability aspects most likely to affect financial performance.

o The *ESG momentum approach,* also called the best-effort (securities) or best-progress (real estate) approach, tilts toward companies that show improvements in ESG measures more quickly than peers.

o The *thematic investing approach* uses positive screening to select companies that solve specific ESG challenges such as climate change and gender diversity.

What is the ESG integration approach to sustainable investing?

ESG integration, also called *integrated investing,* refers to an investment incorporating ESG factors and more traditional financial analysis like cash flow, sales growth, and market share into the securities selection process. Its main objective is to use ESG factors to enhance conventional financial analysis and investment decisions. As a result, ESG investors select companies that demonstrate impressive ESG attributes. Although ESG integration results in a more holistic financial analysis, it still mainly concerns a company's financial performance.

Various approaches to ESG integration are available.

- *Environmental* refers to a company's performance as a steward of the natural environment involving climate change, energy consumption, and pollution.
- *Social* involves how a company manages relationships with its stakeholders such as employees, suppliers, customers, and the communities. Key issues involve diversity, working conditions, safety and health, equal employment opportunities, and local community impact.
- *Governance* deals with a company's management, including ethical business practices, executive compensation, board composition, transparency, and shareholder rights.

Financial performance remains the main objective of integrated investing but with a socially conscious overlay. Investments with good ESG scores may be associated with higher returns, better long-term growth prospects, and reduced risks than those with low ESG scores. Large publicly traded companies often publish reports about their ESG initiatives.

What is the socially responsible investing approach?

Like ESG integration, socially responsible investing (SRI) focuses on publicly traded companies. Yet, unlike ESG integration, SRI looks beyond a company's financial performance. Instead, *SRI* is an investment style that involves actively choosing or removing investments using specific ethical/advocacy guidelines. Traditional SRI investors include or exclude companies based on socially responsible factors such as the nature of the business, its values, how it conducts business, and the "footprint" it leaves on the world. For many investors, these factors are at least as important as the company's profitability. For example, an SRI portfolio could contain investments in companies producing clean technology and low carbon emissions and engaging in gender diversity and local initiatives. Thus, SRI investing goes a step beyond ESG integration.

What are the shareholder engagement and activism approaches to sustainable investing?

Beyond using their values to help select companies for their portfolios, investors can also attempt to influence a public corporation's behavior by exercising their rights as partial owners. Shareholder engagement is particularly relevant for institutional investors because it provides the opportunity to create added value. Activist shareholders can use various tactics to pressure management to bring about change. For example, they can file a *shareholder resolution*, a proposal that shareholders submit for a vote at a company's annual meeting. Such requests typically deal with how management should run the company. However, resolutions can still be helpful without involving a vote. Filing may lead to discussions between those filing a resolution and management. In some instances, the parties can reach agreements leading to withdrawing a resolution.

Other forms of shareholder engagement include attending annual meetings, exercising voting rights, engaging in discussions with corporate management, and joining shareholder coalitions to encourage companies to change their ESG practices. Additionally, investors can engage in offensive tactics, such as using the media to publicize their demands and threatening companies with lawsuits. Finally, shareholder activism can serve as an effective monitoring mechanism to improve corporate governance efficiency and positively impact firm value, performance, and decision making.

What is the sustainable thematic investing approach?

Thematic investing, also called *ESG thematic* and *themed investing*, is an investment approach that attempts to identify macro-level trends and the underlying investments that are likely to benefit if those trends materialize. Investors following a sustainable thematic investing approach focus on economic activities that potentially offer sustainable long-term growth. They create a portfolio or part of a portfolio by identifying companies involved in certain areas (themes) that they predict are likely to generate above-market returns over the long term.

A thematic investment has two characteristics. First, a sustainable company should "do the right thing." That is, it should develop products and services that offer solutions to overcome societal challenges. For example, to address the sustainable theme of clean energy, a company could be involved in renewable energy such as solar, wind, and hydro. Other core areas of thematic investing include climate change, waste and water management, sustainable forestry and agriculture, cybersecurity, artificial intelligence, and health care.

Second, a sustainable company should "do things right." In other words, it should strive to improve the environmental and social impact of its operations. Thus, thematic investing allows investors to address sustainability challenges by investing in companies developing specific solutions to meet such challenges. Thematic investors need to be aware of the difficulty of identifying which themes are likely to be long-term winners and which aren't. Consequently, putting money into thematic investments, including mutual funds and ETFs, involves the chance for high risk and high return.

What is the impact of the investing approach to sustainable investing?

Impact investing is an umbrella term grouping various styles intended to deliver a financial return and positive, measurable social and environmental benefits. The Rockefeller Foundation first coined the term *impact investing* in 2008. Investments are generally project-specific. However, an investment's return is typically subordinate to creating tangible social impact. In the last quarter of the 20th century, impact investing emerged from the corporate social responsibility (CSR) and socially responsible investment movement. Impact investors are more

"Impact investing has become a broad umbrella that includes all investing with a focus on both financial return and social impact, but in its best form, impact investing prioritizes impact over returns and achieves outcomes that traditional investing cannot."

—Jacqueline Novogratz

proactive achieving an impact as opposed to merely avoiding adverse consequences. Thus, impact investing isn't about avoiding the bad but finding and supporting the good.

This investment style intends to help a business or organization complete a project, develop a program, or do something positive to benefit society. Impact investing focuses mainly on social and environmental causes but also extends into other areas. For example, investors practicing impact investing seek to address such challenges as sustainable agriculture, renewable energy, conservation, and affordable and accessible essential services, including housing, health care, and education. Impact investors include foundations, health systems, banks, pension funds, insurance companies, faith-based organizations, corporations, wealth managers, and individuals. However, individual investors may have difficulty gaining access to impact investing through public markets.

To achieve a portfolio with a purpose, you must align your investments with your values and consider factors beyond returns. Some of these factors are hard to quantify. Of course, values differ among investors. For example, some investors want to achieve a cleaner environment, while others seek social justice. Still others desire to promote peace, health, or morality. In summary, socially dimensioned investments attract investors who want a personal connection to their assets and invest in noble causes. The priority attached to financial return differs among socially conscious investors.

What types of investors engage in sustainable investing?

Sustainable investors range from average retail (individual) investors to high-net-worth individuals (accredited investors) and family offices. A *family office* is a private wealth management advisory firm that serves ultra-high-net-worth investors. Others include universities, endowments, foundations, pension funds, religious institutions, nonprofit organizations, sovereign wealth funds, credit unions, community development banks, and venture capitalists. In addition, hundreds of investment management firms invest in funds and other investment vehicles for such investors.

How large is the sustainable investing marketplace?

Sustainable investing is big and getting bigger. According to the Global Sustainable Investment Alliance, sustainable investing grew to more than $30 trillion in 2018. Of this amount, Europe had $14.1 trillion in sustainable investments, followed by $12.0 trillion in the United States. Although Europe has been a leader in ESG investing, the United States is catching up. According to the Bank of America's predictions, another $20 trillion is likely to flow into this area during the next two decades. Thus, ESG investing isn't a fad and is here to stay.

How can investors get started with sustainable investing?

To get started with sustainable investing, you should take the following steps.

- *Get informed.* You need to become knowledgeable about sustainable investing before you invest. You should never invest in an investment vehicle that you don't understand.
- *Choose your nonfinancial criteria.* You also need to be aware of your values. For example, if you're involved in sustainable

"To galvanize the necessary capital to have real impact, sustainable investing can't be limited to investors willing to accept unattractive returns in order to create social good. Getting to scale requires investment products that seek attractive returns while benefiting society."
—James Gorman

investing, you need to articulate what "doing good" means. For example, are you interested in creating a cleaner environment, achieving social justice, or promoting peace, health, and morality? Thus, you need to choose the criteria, such as ESG factors, to analyze a company. ESG are three specific pillars crucial to today's many business managers and investors. A good starting point is to exclude industries you don't want as part of your list of socially responsible enterprises.

- *Choose your financial criteria.* Next, you need to go beyond values and identify the financial criteria necessary to achieve your investment goals. For example, following various ESG strategies no longer comes at the expense of returns; such an approach can be market-beating. Thus, you don't need to compromise your values to make money when engaging in sustainable investing.

- *Identify investments that meet your needs.* You must identify the assets available to meet your goals. The number of choices can be mazelike for newcomers.

- *Compare and choose.* Now you need to sort through your options and select those that best meet your twin goals of profit and purpose. This choice may involve various trade-offs. Regarding the purpose portion of the equation, you might want to use ESG ratings. For example, MSCI ESG Ratings aim to measure a company's resilience to long-term, financially relevant ESG risks. MSCI rates companies on a AAA to CCC scale where CCC and B are laggards; BBB, BB, and A are average; and AA and AAA are leaders. Thus, you should focus on companies in the leader category. Morningstar also has an ESG rating system for mutual funds and ETFs. Morningstar's Portfolio Sustainability Ratings use a five-globe system from one globe (lowest) to five globes (highest) (https://www.investopedia.com/terms/m/morningstar-sustainability-rating.asp).

- *Diversify.* Savvy investors know that you shouldn't put all your eggs in one basket. Therefore, you need to diversify your portfolio to reduce your overall risk.

What vehicles are available for aligning values with investments?

Sustainable investments aren't confined to equities but extend across asset classes. Individual investors can participate in this movement using various investments that match their interests.

> "When it's done right, ESG is good business."
> —Jeremy Richardson

Most investments focus on publicly traded equities in stocks, mutual funds, and ETFs mainly tracking indices. To buy and sell stocks, you'd need to open an account with a broker. However, individual investors often don't want to devote the time required to obtain the necessary knowledge and skill to identify stocks suitable for reaching their goals. Instead, they prefer leaving this task to someone else, such as a mutual fund manager who uses ESG criteria to select stocks, mutual funds, and ETFs.

Although investing in the stock market is the most common choice for individuals engaging in sustainable investing, other options include fixed income securities in the corporate, government, municipal, and other bond sectors that meet sustainable investing principles. For instance, government-issued, mortgage-backed securities (MBS) promote affordable housing, and municipal bonds support local investment. Green bonds are another example. A *green bond* is a fixed income security earmarked to raise money for environmental and climate sustainability projects. Some investors even take an activist approach and engage in a dialogue with issuers.

Besides traditional stocks and bonds, accredited investors can also invest in private equity, emphasizing impact investments. Although the definition varies among countries, an *accredited investor* refers to an individual or a business entity allowed to trade securities that may lack registration with financial authorities. In the United States, accredited investors are high-net-worth or sophisticated investors. They need to have a net worth of more than $1 million, excluding their private residence, or they must have earned income above

$200,000 per year ($300,000 combined with a spouse) for at least three years.

Other asset classes include property funds and real estate investment trusts (REITs) tilted toward sustainable investing and sustainable infrastructure investments. Other options include community investments/development funds such as credit unions, microfinance, and crowdfunding.

What sources are available for evaluating the social responsibility of a good versus bad company?

> "Creating a strong business and building a better world are not conflicting goals—they are both essential ingredients for long-term success."
>
> —Bill Ford

A *socially responsible stock* is the stock of a company that creates social good. That could mean that the company conducts socially positive activities or doesn't do objectionable things. From a sustainability perspective, good companies are often "best-in-class" with healthy, sustainable profiles. They also have sustainable competitive advantages. However, what "good" means differs among investors. Your "good" could be another investor's "bad." Given the complexity of judging a company's ESG profile, numerous rating providers have sprung up to help distinguish between "good" or "bad" socially responsible companies. These providers offer a wide array of data from specialized providers that calculate metrics on specific ESG traits, such as corporate governance or climate, to those that rate companies based on several hundred ESG-related metrics. ESG ratings vary substantially because each provider has a different methodology for assigning company-specific ratings. Because ESG rating systems can evaluate the same company differently, the company's ESG score can

> "We believe an intense focus on sustainability has the potential to deliver returns to investors while also benefiting communities and the environment."
>
> —Katherine Collins

be ranked high by one provider but low by another provider. Using inconsistent methods by ESG data providers can lead to dramatically different outcomes when constructing a portfolio. Investors face many challenges when choosing an ESG rating provider because of the inconsistent, ratings. Thus, you should ensure that the rating provider's approach is consistent with your ESG preferences (https://www.researchaffiliates.com/en_us/publications/articles/what-a-difference-an-esg-ratings-provider-makes.html).

The following websites rate or rank social responsibility.

- *Ethisphere* (https://www.worldsmostethicalcompanies.com). This source offers an annual listing of the World's Most Ethical Companies.
- *Fortune Change the World* (https://fortune.com/change-the-world/) provides an annual ranking of companies that aims to make a profit while making a difference in the world.
- Global 100 (https://www.corporateknights.com/reports/global-100/) provides an index of the Global 100 that ranks the most sustainable corporations in the world.

Other databases such as Mergent Online, CSRHub, MSCI, S&P Global, Sustainalytics, and Vigeo Eirisare are also available but typically involve a subscription. However, some libraries may have access to these sources.

What are the pros and cons of investing in ESG stocks?

Common stock represents part ownership of publicly traded companies. Owning ESG stocks offers both pros and cons.

- *Pros.* On the positive side, stocks provide the potential for higher returns than other types of investments, such as bonds, over the long term but are often riskier. By engaging in sustainable investing, you have the added satisfaction of doing good. As a partial owner, you may influence the company through shareholder votes. Additionally, if you have strong ties with a stock, you're likely to stick with it for the longer term.

- *Cons.* On the negative side, no single criterion exists for making a company socially sustainable. A company can be socially sustainable in one area but not in others. You can also lose money by investing in ESG stocks. You're the last to get paid because companies aren't required to pay dividends, and you're last in line behind other creditors in bankruptcy proceedings. Also, exercising control over your investment can be difficult, if not impossible.

What are some examples of the largest ESG stocks?

If you want to invest in ESG stocks, the list is extensive and depends on what specific ESG criteria you plan to use. Below is a list of the largest ESG stocks in market capitalization in the MSCI World SRI Index in 2020. The index includes companies with outstanding ESG ratings and excludes companies whose products have negative social or environmental impacts.

- *Microsoft Corp.* (NASDAQ: MSFT) is the largest company following ESG practices globally. This American company is in the information technology (IT) sector and makes personal and business software.
- *Tesla* (NASDAQ: TSLA) is an American electric vehicle and clean energy company.
- *Procter & Gamble Company* (NYSE: PG) is an American multinational consumer goods corporation.
- *NVIDIA* (NASDAQ: NVDA) is an American multinational technology company that designs graphics processing units for the gaming and professional markets.
- *Home Depot, Inc.* (NYSE: HD) is the largest home improvement retailer in the United States, supplying tools, construction products, and services.

- *Roche Holding AG* (SIX Swiss Exchange: RO and OTCQX: RHHBY) is a Swiss company that develops and manufactures pharmaceutical and diagnostic products.
- *Walt Disney Company* (NYSE: DIS) is an American company and one of the world's leading entertainment and information providers.
- *Salesforce.com* (NYSE: CRM) is an American cloud-based software company providing customer relationship management service and sells a complementary suite of enterprise applications focused on customer service, marketing automation, analytics, and application development.
- *PepsiCo* (NASDAQ: PEP) is an American multinational food, snack, and beverage corporation that manufactures, markets, and distributes grain-based snack foods, beverages, and other products.
- *SAP* (NYSE: SAP) is a German multinational software corporation that makes enterprise software to manage business operations and customer relations.

What are the pros and cons of mutual funds and exchange-traded funds engaged in sustainable investing?

Mutual funds and exchange-traded funds (ETFs) engaging in sustainable investing are portfolios of equities or bonds that integrate ESG factors into the investment process.

"More investors I think are starting to understand that they can use ESG funds, sustainable funds across their entire portfolio."
—Jon Hale

- *Pros.* Individual investors generally prefer investing in such funds instead of individual stocks and bonds because they provide diversification, professional management, and low required minimum investments. As a result, investors can choose funds that reflect their values. Additionally, some investors may develop an attachment for such funds and stick with them through market turbulence, a valuable behavioral component for long-term investors.

- *Cons.* However, these funds aren't one-size-fits-all, so you need to ensure that a fund's core values are consistent with your own. For instance, one fund may emphasize the "E," while another focuses on the "S" or "G" in ESG. Additionally, thematic ETFs can have greater volatility and risk, particularly in trendy niche categories. You may also find that the costs and ongoing fees can be slightly higher for these funds than traditional ones. Finally, achieving strong performance isn't a slam dunk.

What are the similarities and differences between mutual funds and ETFs engaged in sustainable investing?

A *mutual fund* is an open-end investment company that pools money from many investors and invests it on their behalf based on a particular investing strategy. Because mutual funds are open-ended, trading occurs between investors and the fund, and the number of shares available is limitless. An *ETF* is an investment company whose shares trade at market-determined prices. As a result, it has a limited number of shares. Mutual funds based on ESG criteria have been available for decades. Pax World launched the first sustainable mutual fund (PAXWX) in 1971. The Domini 400 Social Index, now named MSCI KLD 400 Social Index, was established in 1990 and was the first capitalization-weighted index built to track sustainable investments.

Mutual funds and ETFs share some standard features but have distinct differences.

- *Similarities.* One similarity is that they purportedly go through a screening process to meet the fund's goals involving various factors, including ESG. Professional money managers oversee both mutual funds and ETFs. Both have built-in diversification, making them less risky than investing in individual stocks, bonds, and other investment options.

Managers of these funds can use an active or passive approach. An *actively managed investment fund* is a fund in which a manager or a management team decides how to invest

"The best way to own common stocks is through an index fund."
—Warren Buffett

the fund's money to beat the market. A *passively managed fund,* also called an *index fund,* is designed to track a market index's performance. It doesn't have a management team making investment decisions on buying and selling individual stocks and bonds. Thus, it doesn't try to beat the market but match it. Actively managed funds are usually mutual funds, but most ETFs are index funds.

- *Differences.* Investors can trade ETFs like stocks, but they can only buy mutual funds at the end of each trading day based on a calculated price called the *net asset value* (NAV). *NAV* is the value of a mutual fund share reached by deducting the fund's liabilities from the market value of all its shares and dividing by the number of issued shares. In addition, mutual funds typically have higher fees and expense ratios than ETFs, partly reflecting the higher costs of being actively managed and a higher minimum investment requirement.

What are the different types of funds engaging in sustainable investing and examples of each?

Perhaps the most basic approach is to buy mutual funds or ETFs engaged in sustainable investing strategies. Figure 4.2 shows several classes of such funds.

- *Negative/exclusionary screening.* Many funds involved in sustainable investing avoid companies that do business in controversial areas. For example, Vanguard FTSE Social Index Fund Admiral Shares (VFTAX) is a mutual fund that excludes companies' stocks in the following industries: adult entertainment, alcohol, fossil fuels,

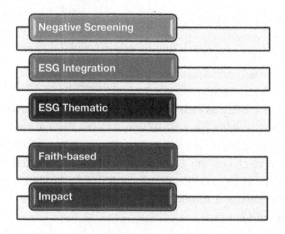

Figure 4.2 Mutual Funds and ETFs Engaging in Sustainable Investing Strategies

gambling, nuclear power, tobacco, and weapons. It also ignores companies that don't meet the UN global compact principles' standards and specific diversity criteria. Examples of exclusionary ETFs are iShares MSCI KLD 400 Social ETF (DSI), Vanguard ESG US Stock ETF (ESGV), and Vanguard ESG International Stock ETF (VSGX). However, just because a fund excludes a company using a negative screen doesn't guarantee that the companies included in the fund don't engage in other objectionable practices.

- *ESG integration.* These funds incorporate ESG factors into investment decisions to help better identify risks and opportunities. For example, the Parnassus Core Equity Fund (PRBLX) is one of the largest ETFs focusing on ESG and sustainability principles. It invests in U.S. large-cap companies with long-term competitive advantages and relevancy, quality management teams, and positive performance on ESG criteria. TIAA-CREF Social Choice Equity Fund (TISCX) is a large mutual fund investing mainly in U.S. companies with leadership in ESG performance relative to their peers. Two other examples are the Fidelity® US Sustainability Index Fund (FITLX) and Fidelity® International Sustainability Index Fund (FNIDX). Both mutual funds are index funds tracking a benchmark that targets high ESG ratings, while maintaining broad market exposure. The first fund is a U.S. equity index fund, and the second fund tracks an international stock benchmark. A final example is the Vanguard Global ESG Select Stock Fund (VEIGX). This actively managed fund seeks to invest in global mid-cap and large-cap companies with high financial productivity and leading ESG practices.

- *ESG thematic.* These funds focus on long-term themes broadly tied to specific areas of sustainability. One environmental theme attracting substantial attention is green investing, ranging from green energy (water, wind, and solar) to green transportation. For example, the Fidelity® Water Sustainability Fund (FLOWX) invests in companies helping to deliver safe, reliable, and easily accessible water. Another example is the iShares MSCI ACWI Low Carbon Target ETF (CRBN), a sustainable ETF focusing on low carbon emissions companies. Several social and governance-focused funds include the Fidelity® Women's Leadership Fund (FWOMX) and Pax Ellevate Global Women's Index Fund (PXWIX), investing in companies that prioritize women's leadership and development.

- *Faith-based funds.* Faith-based funds invest according to Catholic, Islamic, Jewish, and Protestant values. For example, the S&P 500 Catholic Values ETF (CATH) provides exposure to companies approved by the United States Conference of Catholic Bishops. The Ave Maria Growth Fund (AVEGX) seeks long-term capital appreciation from equity investments in companies that follow the Roman Catholic Church's core values and teachings. This fund avoids companies with ties to abortion or pornography. The Ave Maria Bond (AVEFX) is a fixed-income fund option. Other funds follow Islamic, or Shariah, finance principles, including Amana Income

(AMANX), excluding companies involved in alcohol, pork, gambling, pornography, tobacco, or other so-called sin stocks.

- *Impact funds.* An *impact fund* is an investment intended to generate a financial return and a positive and measurable impact on specific social or environmental objectives. For example, the FlexShares STOXX US ESG Impact Index Fund (ESG) seeks enhanced risk-return characteristics relative to the broad large-cap U.S. equity market by tracking a custom index, the STOXX USA ESG Impact Index. Domini has four impact funds.

  o The Domini Impact Equity Fund (DSEFX) is a diversified stock portfolio seeking long-term total returns to promote universal human dignity and ecological sustainability.

  o The Domini Impact International Equity Fund (DOMIX) invests primarily in stocks of companies in Europe, the Asia-Pacific region, and other areas that meet Domini Impact Investments' social and environmental standards.

  o The Domini Sustainable Solutions Fund (CAREX) invests in companies that develop and provide access to solution-oriented products and services such as renewable energy systems and electric vehicles.

  o The Domini Impact Bond Fund (DSBFX) invests at least 80% of its assets in investment-grade fixed-income securities.

What options are available for socially responsible investors interested in fixed-income investments?

Socially responsible investors can place their money in individual bonds, bond mutual funds, and bond ETFs. A *bond* is a form of a loan from a private investor to a company or government. Unlike stocks, bonds don't grant the owner any ownership stake. Instead, they promise to pay interest, except a zero-coupon bond, and they repay the principal to the owner.

Unlike ordinary bonds, issuers use the money generated from green bonds for environmentally friendly projects. Bonds are available from the corporate, government, and municipal sectors. Bond funds engaging in sustainable investing are multifaceted. Some are broadly diversified index funds that purchase bonds from issuers with solid ESG practices. Others are actively managed funds engaging with corporate and municipal issuers to fund ESG-related projects and more specialized offerings, such as funds that buy environmentally focused "green" bonds.

Here are some examples of bond funds involved in SRI.

- *Fidelity® Sustainability Bond Index Fund (FNDSX)* is a bond index mutual fund tracking a benchmark that comprises investment-grade government, corporate, and asset-backed securities from issuers with robust sustainability profiles.
- *Invesco Taxable Municipal Bond Portfolio ETF (NYSE: BAB)* allows investors to fund environmentally friendly projects and manage risk through bonds from local municipalities.
- *iShares GNMA Bond ETF (NASDAQ: GNMA)* offers investors a chance to "promote affordable housing" through investments in residential mortgage-backed bonds issued by the US government.
- *SPDR SSGA Gender Diversity Index ETF (NYSE: SHE)* seeks exposure to U.S. companies that demonstrate greater gender diversity within senior leadership than other firms in their sector.
- *Vanguard ESG US Corporate Bond ETF (CBOE/BATS: VCEB)* seeks to track the performance of the Bloomberg Barclays MSCI US Corporate SRI Select Index.

What are green bonds and their pros and cons?

A *green bond* is a debt instrument designed to raise funds for projects and businesses with a positive environmental or social impact. Green bond issuers use the proceeds for "green"

> "Green bonds as a device may be a stepping stone, or maybe a milestone, on a journey to the bringing together of trillions of dollars that are necessary to map these issues and challenges we have."
>
> —Dave Chen

projects, assets, or business activities with environmental benefits such as providing power generation systems, preventing pollution, protecting ecosystems, and offering clean transportation. The European Investment Bank first issued green bonds in 2007, followed by the World Bank in 2008. The green bond market has experienced rapid expansion since its conception. The growth in green bonds largely stems from the increasing importance of climate change.

Most green bonds are structurally identical to conventional bonds but have a disclosed "green" use of the proceeds. Green bonds come in six forms: (1) corporate bond, (2) municipal bond, (3) project bond, (4) financial sector bond, (5) asset-backed security, and (6) supranational, subsovereign, and agency (SSA) bond.

Although individual investors can buy individual green bonds, they typically are better off purchasing a green bond fund or ETF. Below are a few examples of such funds.

- *Calvert Green Bond A (CGAFX)* is a fund that isn't limited to bonds labeled as green but focuses on three broad types of issuers: green projects, solutions providers, and environmental leaders.
- *VanEck Vectors® Green Bond ETF (NYSE: GRNB)* invests in bonds designated as "green" by the Climate Bonds Initiative issued to finance projects that positively impact the environment.
- *iShares Global Green Bond ETF (NASDAQ: BGRN)* seeks to track the investment results of an index composed of global investment-grade green bonds issued to fund environmental projects.

As with any investment, green bonds have pros and cons from the investor's perspective.

- *Pros.* On the positive side, green bonds give investors the chance to profit while supporting positive ESG causes. These bonds are often less sensitive to the health of the overall economy and provide diversification benefits. As the green bond market matures, greater issuer diversification by sector and geography becomes available. Green bonds are tax-exempt if a municipality or government organization issues them and uses the bond proceeds to finance a physical property's construction. Hence, they offer tax advantages for savvy investors.
- *Cons.* Investing in green bonds isn't without risks. One disadvantage of green bond investing is liquidity due to the market's relatively small size. Also, there's no standardized definition of the meaning of "green," despite voluntary attempts to resolve this issue. The broad scope of what constitutes a "green" bond suggests that investors may or may not know where their money goes. Thus, greenwashing's potential problem occurs without common, agreed-upon global standards and legislation concerning green bonds. As previously noted, *greenwashing* refers to activities by a company or an organization intended to make people believe that it's concerned about the environment when the only genuine concern is making money. Transparency in the "use of proceeds" is the key to market integrity. Other potential drawbacks include low yields, insufficient research, and mispricing.

What are social impact bonds and their benefits and challenges?

A *social impact bond* (SIB), also called a *pay for success* or *social benefit bond*, is a financial security providing capital for public-sector projects intended to create better social outcomes and lead to savings. It involves a multiparty contract between governments seeking financial support for innovative programs and policies and investors with money to lend them.

It's a relatively new development in finance first introduced in the United Kingdom in 2010. SIBs align the interests of various parties—governments, investors, and others—to develop practical solutions for public-sector problems involving the environment, social welfare, education, criminal justice, employment, and other areas.

Despite being called a bond, a SIB isn't a bond in the traditional sense. It has some features of a conventional bond but lacks others. For example, like a typical bond, a SIB has a fixed term. However, it doesn't sell in capital markets, offer a fixed rate of return to investors, or provide intermediate cash flow during the project's life. Instead, investors receive the cash flow—repayment of principal plus any potential profit—at the end of the maturity period if the underlying project is successful. An independent evaluator assesses a project's success using predetermined metrics. Assuming a project meets these criteria, the government pays the project manager, who then transfers the funds to the SIB investors.

The United States' first SIB was a recidivism program focused on helping adolescent Rikers Island inmates stay out of trouble through education and counseling. Unfortunately, this project failed to meet its benchmarks. However, the second U.S. social impact bond program, which dealt with early childhood education in Salt Lake County, Utah, achieved a 99% success rate in reducing the need for special education in elementary school. Hence, the private funds provided through SIBs can bring about government social changes without taxpayers bearing the program's costs. In theory, SIBs are a win-win—improved social outcomes save governments money while investors receive a return on their capital—but only if a project is successful. So far, SIBs have a mixed track record of success.

- *Benefits*. SIBs raise capital for vital social services without using tax dollars. Thus, they bring new sources of capital to nonprofit programs, providing social programs with an opportunity to grow to scale. They also increase incentives for nonprofits to focus on productivity and outcomes.

- *Challenges.* SIBS have their critics. For example, some claim that they may be promoting simplistic solutions to complex problems. SIBs also come with challenges and risks to investors. For example, these multiparty financial investments are complicated and involve high implementation costs. Measuring the program's effectiveness to society and determining the payback to investors are difficult.

Perhaps the main risk of these performance-based investments is that investors bear all the risks. Given the current lack of an active secondary market for SIBs, investors face high liquidity risks. Moreover, repayment to investors depends on achieving specified social outcomes. If a project fails, they don't receive anything, including the principal. SIBs also don't receive any preferential tax treatment despite providing a societal benefit. Additionally, some social impact programs require a long time to create societal benefits.

How can investors use ESG target-date funds?

If you're looking for a socially responsible option in your retirement plan, such as a 401(k) plan, an ESG target-date mutual fund (TDF) could interest you. According to one source, nearly 90% of employer-sponsored defined contribution plans offer a TDF. A *defined contribution plan* is a retirement plan where an employer, employee, or both regularly contribute. Such funds are among the most popular default investment options used by 401(k) participants. A *target-date fund*, also called a *lifecycle fund*, is a class of mutual funds that periodically rebalances a portfolio to meet an investor's retirement

"Target-date funds are designed to age with you by automatically rebalancing your portfolio from growth investments toward more conservative ones as retirement nears."

—Kevin Voigt

date. Think of it as a type of all-in-one fund. TDFs are available at every major broker under various names. For example, Fidelity calls them Freedom Funds, Vanguard refers to them as Target Retirement Funds, and Charles Schwab labels them Target Date Funds.

Some TDFs include ESG criteria in selecting the investments to hold in the portfolio. For example, a fund starts with a larger percentage of ESG stocks when you're younger and gradually increases the percentage of ESG bonds and other low-risk investments as you age. With this simple investment solution, the portfolio's asset allocation mix becomes more conservative as the target date approaches. Thus, target-date portfolio managers use the target date to determine the fund's risk level and readjust the level annually.

A TDF can take you "to" or "through" retirement. A "to retirement" TDF reaches its most conservative asset allocation on the target date, say 2040. Following that date, the fund's allocation typically remains unchanged throughout retirement. A "through retirement" TDF continues to rebalance and usually reaches its most conservative asset allocation after the target date. Some TDFs merge into a "retirement" or "income" fund that typically focuses on generating income upon reaching their target dates. For example, Natixis Sustainable Future Funds® appeal to retirement investors who want sustainable long-term returns. The funds combine a sophisticated "through retirement" allocation glide path focusing on ESG investing. A *glide path* refers to a formula that defines the TDF's strategic asset allocation mix based on the number of years to the target date. It changes the asset allocation among higher-risk and lower-risk assets over the time horizon.

What are the advantages and disadvantages of ESG TDFs?

Although the first TDFs started in the early 1990s, Natixis Global Asset Management created the first set of sustainable

TDFs in 2016 with five-year vintages ranging from target dates of 2015 to 2060. Natixis Sustainable Future Funds use a mix of active and passive investment strategies to invest in ESG-minded companies that focus on areas such as population growth, increasing urbanization, an aging population, technical breakthroughs, and climate change. However, despite the attractiveness of ESG to investors, most TDFs holding the majority of 401(k) plan assets don't incorporate ESG.

ESG TDFs have both benefits and drawbacks.

- *Advantages.* On the positive side, TDFs are long-term investments with a particular retirement date in mind. In addition, they offer low minimums, professionally managed portfolios, automatic rebalancing, broad diversification, and low maintenance because they're a one-size-fits-all solution. These "set it and forget it" investments are on autopilot because the portfolio manager decides the asset mix and adjusts it over time. Thus, ESG TDFs are well suited for busy investors who want to avoid the time and hassle of making ongoing investment decisions.
- *Disadvantages.* On the negative side, the creators of TDFs design them for the "average person." Not all retirements are the same. Reaching the target date doesn't mean you've saved enough to meet your goal. If your chosen retirement year's asset allocation isn't consistent with your risk tolerance, you should select another target-date year.

TDFs charge higher fees than other passive investments due to active management. Therefore, someone must determine the asset allocations. TDFs also don't guarantee income and capital gains. Because these funds are one-size-fits-all investments, they lack flexibility if your needs or goals change. TDFs may also be too conservative because some may have a large allocation in bonds. Moreover, these funds base their weighting on your retirement year, not your "finish line," meaning they don't automatically adjust for any risk or return preferences you may have after retirement.

What are some tips in selecting an ESG TDF?

> "All the time and effort that people devote to picking the right fund, the hot hand, the great manager, have in most cases led to no advantage."
>
> —Peter Lynch

The Financial Industry Regulatory Authority (FINRA) offers the following tips on choosing a TDF (https://www.finra.org/investors/learn-to-invest/types-investments/retirement/target-date-funds-find-right-target-you).

- *Pick your target date carefully.* You should select a target date, usually close to your retirement date but aligned closely with your retirement investment strategy.
- *Assess how much risk you're willing to take.* You should select a target date that best matches your risk tolerance. Remember that your circumstances could change.
- *Determine whether the fund takes you to or through retirement.* You should decide whether you want the fund to reach its most conservative asset allocation on or after the target date.
- *Monitor the glide path of your TDF.* Because TDFs have different glide paths, you need to make sure the glide path is right for you.
- *Keep your "mixed" investments balanced.* For example, if a TDF is only part of your investment portfolio, you should be comfortable with your overall asset allocation and rebalance periodically based on your needs.
- *Check fees and expenses.* You should compare the overall costs of TDFs to find the one that provides the best trade-offs. A slight difference in these costs can substantially impact your TDF's returns over time.

What are the trade-offs between investing in stocks or bonds of socially responsible companies, mutual funds, and ETFs?

When investing in stocks or bonds, you must identify the specific securities you want to own. Taking a do-it-yourself (DIY) approach to sustainable investing assures that the companies included in your portfolio support your values. If you decide to take this path, you need to open a brokerage account before buying and selling securities. You also need to screen your investments with care. Examples of discount brokerage firms attractive for socially responsible investors include Charles Schwab and E*Trade because of their supporting investment tools.

Nonetheless, the burden of selecting securities for your portfolio rests with you. Typically, individual investors don't want to invest the time and effort needed to analyze and choose individual stocks or bonds. After all, not everyone is a great analyst or stock picker.

If you're not a DIY investor, you have several choices. One option is to seek the help of a financial advisor who can provide an independent and objective view of your money and how you're using it. Such advisors provide customized, holistic solutions and offer investment options. Working with financial advisors is particularly useful if you have complex financial issues. You're generally better off working with a qualified, fee-only (not commission-based) advisor who is a fiduciary, especially if you're a novice. A *fiduciary* is someone bound both legally and ethically to act in your best interests. However, financial advisors aren't free, and many require a minimum investment amount that could be beyond your reach.

Another option is to use a fund manager. Why? The reasons are straightforward—the advantages of engaging in sustainable funds outweigh the time, effort, and energy required to construct a well-diversified ESG portfolio. The best advice is to invest in passively managed mutual funds and ETFs for the typical individual investor who lacks a strong background and interest in investments. These index funds provide low-cost portfolio diversification without the hassle. However, you will need a brokerage account to purchase ETFs because they're bought and sold like stocks. Most actively managed mutual funds don't beat their benchmarks, so identifying those likely to do so in the future is difficult. Past performance doesn't guarantee future results.

What are robo-advisors and the trade-offs of using them for sustainable investing?

If you're a hands-off investor, another option is to use a *robo-advisor*. This automated online investment platform relies on computers instead of human financial advisors to build and manage your portfolio. First, you receive financial advice based on mathematical rules or algorithms. Then, the software uses its algorithms to allocate, manage, and optimize your assets automatically.

> "Robo-advisors are best for novice investors who want a simplified, automated, affordable way to grow their money."
>
> —Colin Lalley

The concept of robo-advisors is like the idea behind TDFs. Both provide one-stop shopping for your entire investment portfolio. However, instead of having you analyze various TDFs to find the one that best meets your needs, a robo-advisor asks you a series of questions and then chooses for you. However, robo-advisors often cost more than other all-in-one funds, such as TDFs.

- *Advantages.* Although not everyone wants to receive digital advice, robo-advisors offer several benefits, especially for entry-level investors, due to their low fees, low-cost threshold, and ease of use. Many robo-advisors keep costs down by following optimized indexed investing strategies in index mutual funds and

ETFs. This approach is best suited for most individual investors. Robo-advisors offer the same investor benefits on socially responsible portfolios as they do with general investing portfolios. For example, you can select your investment asset allocations, rebalance your portfolio, and reinvest dividends. Some robo-advisors offer *tax-loss harvesting*, which involves selling securities at a loss to offset a capital gains tax liability. Because robo-advisors put sustainable investing within reach of investors at all levels, they're an excellent option to help you get started.

- *Disadvantages.* Although robo-advisors are a great innovation, they have several drawbacks. First, they provide services not financial planning, which financial planners and advisors perform. Second, robo-advisor fees are on top of those of the underlying fund. For example, robo-advisors often charge around 0.25%, but many low-cost index funds charge less than 0.10%.

What are some examples of robo-advisors for sustainable investing?

If you're interested in sustainable investing, here are some highly rated robo-advisors to consider (https://www.money under30.com/best-robo-advisors-for-socially-responsible-investing). Betterment, Personal Capital, and Wealthsimple are general investment platforms that offer a portfolio service involving sustainable investments, whereas Earthfolio focuses exclusively on sustainable investments.

- *Betterment* (https://www.betterment.com) is a leader among robo-advisors and concentrates its sustainable investments in two asset classes—U.S. large-cap stocks and emerging market stocks—and invests only in low-cost index-based ETFs for those two asset classes. In addition, Betterment offers two options: Betterment Digital has no account minimum and charges 0.25% of assets under management (AUM) annually; Betterment Premium provides unlimited phone access to certified financial planners for a 0.40% fee and a $100,000 account minimum.

- *Personal Capital* (https://www.personalcapital.com) focuses on high-net-worth individuals with a $100,000 minimum investment. Each portfolio consists of domestic and international equities and bonds, alternative investments, and cash. Personal Capital uses a "best-in-class" selection of companies within broad indices and excludes specific energy, gambling, and tobacco-related industries. It charges 0.89% per year of AUM for most investors.

- *Wealthsimple* (https://www.wealthsimple.com/en-us/) is a Canadian online investment management service focused on millennials. It offers a diverse lineup of portfolio choices, including socially responsible options. Investors can choose from three risk-weighted portfolios (conservative, balanced, and growth) drawn from six ETFs involved with sustainable investments. It has a $0 account minimum and a 0.40–0.50% advisory fee, making it on the pricier side of the competition. In addition, its investment expense ratio is 0.25% on portfolios engaged in sustainable investing, higher than 0.09–0.12% on standard portfolios.

- *Earthfolio* (https://www.earthfolio.net) is the world's first automated investment service dedicated to sustainable investing. Using time-tested strategies and modern portfolio theory, managers at Earthfolio create an asset allocation designed to meet your specific goals and risk tolerance. Earthfolio allocates and diversifies your money across a broad selection of mutual funds dedicated to sustainable investments but doesn't use ETFs for the asset classes. The minimum investment is $25,000, and it charges a fee of 0.50% per year of your account balance.

What is community investing?

Community investing seeks to finance projects or institutions that serve poor and underserved communities, primarily low-income individuals, small businesses, and community services such as health care, affordable housing, and childcare. It involves direct investments into these communities through community development financial institutions (CDFIs). CDFIs include community development loan funds (CDLFs), community development banks (CDBs), credit unions (CDCUs), and community development corporations (CDCs). Investments can be cash deposits in community banks, purchasing debt from nonprofit loan funds, and equity investments in real estate. CDLFs are private financial institutions that provide financing and development services to underserved and often low-income communities. The main types of loan funds—microenterprise, small business, housing, and community service organizations—are loaned out in a specific geographic area. A *microenterprise* is a business operating on a tiny scale. Although these loans are safe and have steady interest payments, the interest rates are generally low, and the Federal Deposit Insurance Corporation (FDIC) doesn't provide insurance for most loan funds. Additionally, not all loan funds accept investments from individuals. A CDFI locator tool (https://ofn.org/cdfi-locator) is available to find a CDLF in specific areas in the United States.

- *CDBs* and *CDCUs* are financial institutions that focus on serving low-income communities lacking access to the traditional financial system.
- *CDCs* are nonprofit organizations created to support and revitalize communities.

Various types of high-impact community investing opportunities are available for individual investors. For example, you can place your money in a certificate of deposit (CD) in a CDFI bank or credit union that lends to individuals and businesses that otherwise couldn't get a loan. You can also buy Calvert Foundation Community Notes that

"Investing for the poor requires participation from the entire community."
—Bill Gates

invest the money through CDFIs around the country. These notes are available through major brokerage houses and Calvert Impact Capital. In addition, some socially responsible mutual funds have a community investment component.

Another form of community investing is to buy municipal bonds in underserved communities and bonds issued by government agencies and government-sponsored enterprises (GSEs). Examples of such agencies include the Government National Mortgage Association (Ginnie Mae), and GSEs include the Federal National Mortgage Association (Fannie Mae) and the Federal Home Loan Mortgage Corporation (Freddie Mac). These entities provide housing to people who otherwise couldn't afford it.

Other types of community investing are also available. One option includes investing in a microenterprise loan fund designed to provide small loans and training to entrepreneurs. Another option is to invest in a community development venture capital (CDVC) fund offering loans and equity capital to businesses in underinvested markets. Finally, a less direct way to be involved in community investing is to buy stock in publicly traded companies that invest in underserved communities. In summary, although community investments aren't necessarily the best way to grow your wealth, they offer a way to improve local communities and diversify your portfolio.

What are online sources of information for sustainable investing?

Many websites are available that provide information on sustainable investing. Below are a few of them.

- *Social Funds* (https://www.socialfunds.com) is the largest personal finance site devoted to SRI. SocialFunds. com features over 10,000 pages of information on mutual funds, community investments, corporate research, shareowner actions, and daily social investment news involving SRI.

- *The Forum for Sustainable and Responsible Investment (US SIF)* (https://www.ussif.org) is a US-based membership association located in Washington, DC, advancing RSII across all asset classes.
- *SRI-CONNECT* (https://www.sri-connect.com) is the online global marketplace for socially responsible and corporate governance research. It provides practical research resources and communication channels to accelerate sustainability factors in "mainstream" analysis and investment.
- *The Global Impact Investing Network* (GIIN) (https://thegiin.org) is a nonprofit organization dedicated to increasing the scale and effectiveness of impact investing. Impact investments are investments made into companies, organizations, and funds to generate social and environmental impact alongside a financial return.

Takeaways

Today, many investors aren't satisfied with merely realizing competitive financial returns. They also want their investments to reflect their values and generate a positive impact. Moreover, these investors believe in using their money to contribute to advancements in ESG practices. Thus, they're motivated to achieve the dual goals of profit and purpose. This fact is evident because sustainable investing is hot, with no signs of cooling off.

Various approaches or strategies are available to attain the goals of making money while doing good. Investors concerned with sustainable investing can invest in multiple products and asset classes, including public equity investments (stocks), fixed income, cash equivalents, and alternative investments. Savvy investors know that they don't necessarily have to sacrifice financial performance to realize their values. However, some are willing to do so. Research shows that companies with strong corporate social responsibility policies and practices can make sound investments.

If you plan to engage in sustainable investing, here are some key takeaways from this chapter.

- Identify your values before engaging in sustainable investing.
- Understand your risk tolerance before investing.
- Consider sustainable investment returns and risks.
- Adopt a sustainable investing approach that's right for you.
- Be sure a company's or fund's objectives and strategies match your profit and purpose investment goals.
- Use mutual funds and ETFs, especially index funds, to diversify your portfolio quickly, cheaply, and conveniently.
- Consider using an ESG target-date retirement fund.

Note: The companies, funds, and other investments mentioned in this chapter are examples to help you begin your research, not investment recommendations.

5

PERFORMANCE IMPLICATIONS OF SUSTAINABLE INVESTING

CAN YOU HAVE YOUR CAKE AND EAT IT TOO?

We need to start to talk about money in ways that dethrone it and make it subject to human ethics and standards of love and decency.

—Joel Solomon

Sustainable investing involves two performance issues. The first is financial performance, which consists of comparing sustainable investments to traditional investments. The second is social performance, which is harder to measure and implies an actual benefit to society. Does sustainable investing change leadership at the corporate level? Do today's business royalty, like Jeff Bezos of Amazon, Elon Musk of Tesla, and Mark Zuckerberg of Meta, care about all stakeholders, not just shareholders?

If the answer is "yes," this response would represent a radical change in leadership. For much of recorded history, the rich have often ignored the plight of the poor. Even from an academic perspective, business schools around the globe have taught business leaders to focus on one thing above all else—increasing the company's stock price and hence shareholder wealth. As a result, shareholders have historically come

> "Let them eat cake."
> —Probably not Marie Antoinette

before other stakeholders. If the other stakeholders complain, they can just "eat cake."

The phrase "Let them eat cake" conveys much about the relationship between the rich and the poor. Historians often attribute the phrase to Marie Antoinette, the Queen of France during the late 18th century. Although she probably never spoke the phrase, those four words have come to represent the events leading to the infamous French Revolution. For starters, the phrase is a rough translation of the French phrase "Qu'ils mangent de la brioche," referring to a fancy type of bread made with a generous amount of eggs and butter. This distinction is vital because regular bread was already an expensive staple in the eyes of French commoners at that time, costing, by some accounts, around 50% of their total income. Therefore, "Let them eat cake" depicts the Queen's hypothetical response to starving peasants facing a severe bread shortage during a brutal famine. Her solution was simple: the peasants should just buy more expensive brioche instead.

Thus, to this day, the phrase "Let them eat cake" is usually interpreted as a leader's absolute ignorance or disregard of the starvation and plight of others. In that context, mistakenly attributing the quote to Marie Antoinette makes sense. By most accounts, she lived a luxurious life, and the French people disliked her. She was so unpopular that her fate was to be beheaded after what was most likely a predetermined verdict in her trial by the Revolutionary Tribunal. This group declared that she was guilty of treason, conspiracy, and depletion of the national treasury. The punishment was severe, but the French

> "I have ever believed that, had there been no Queen, there would have been no revolution."
> —Thomas Jefferson

people viewed her as a poor leader. In today's terms, she would have been a bad choice for a company's chief executive officer (CEO), given that she was oblivious to the needs of most French stakeholders.

Much has happened since the 18th century. For one thing, bad leaders no longer face losing their heads these days. Even France finally abandoned using the guillotine in 1981. Fortunately, people today prefer more civilized ways to get their messages across. The phrase "Let them eat cake" has taken on great symbolic importance since the French Revolution that followed Marie Antoinette's death. And as was the case with the French Revolution, an investor revolution is ongoing today to hold leaders, especially CEOs of major corporations, accountable. That revolution has a name—sustainable investing!

Coincidentally, sustainable investing began to take off not long after France officially stopped using the guillotine. Although some sustainable investment opportunities were available in the 1980s and early 1990s, sustainable investing increased its momentum in the United States around the mid-1990s. As evidence, sustainable investing rose in the United States from $639 billion assets under management (AUM) in 1995 to $17.1 trillion AUM in 2020, more than 25 times its size 25 years earlier. More impressive, most of that growth (roughly $14 trillion) came in the last decade. Moreover, professional investors—not naïve investors—primarily hold sustainable investments. A total of 384 money managers, 530 institutional investors, and 1,204 community-focused investment institutions possess the most U.S. sustainable assets. However, substantial crossover exists between these groups. For example, money managers on behalf of institutional investors hold over 70% of these assets or about $12 trillion (SIF, 2020).

Sustainable investing's growth links to the expanding choir of practitioner voices singing its praises in many ways. They often claim that sustainable investment products offer social returns and provide competitive financial returns similar to traditional investment products. Many academics agree. An expanding body of research has concluded that sustainable investors don't face a financial trade-off for incorporating screening criteria like environmental, social, and governance

(ESG) factors into their portfolios. However, some disagreement exists.

This chapter examines research on sustainable investing. It also discusses research that attempts to break the tie between favoring sustainable investing and supporting traditional investing. Unlike other chapters in this book, here we discuss various studies and provide a list of references at the end of the book, enabling you to review these studies in more depth if you choose.

The chapter begins by examining how to measure sustainable funds. The remainder of the chapter discusses the performance of equity funds, indices, fixed income, and "sin" stocks. It also explores the impact of sustainable investing on corporate behavior. By the end of this chapter, you should gain an overall perspective on sustainable investing performance, especially compared to more traditional options. Finally, the chapter looks at the old English idiom, "You can't eat your cake and have it too," meaning you can't simultaneously retain the cake and also eat it. In other words, you can't have it both ways. In many circumstances, this saying is true. However, sustainable investing might be an exception to the rule. Sustainable investors want to know whether they can retain their financial returns and get a social return at the same time. You can decide for yourself if you "can have your cake (or fancy bread) and eat it too."

What are the supply and demand dynamics for performance data for sustainable investing?

With the amount of attention that sustainable investing has received, proper measurement of performance and tracking has also gained attention. The most common approach to sustainable investing is ESG integration, which evaluates stocks through an ESG lens alongside traditional performance metrics like cash flow and capital allocation (Stevens, 2019). Morgan Stanley (2020a) gathered global survey data from 110 large asset owners, including financial institutions, insurers, and pensions. The data show that an estimated 95% of these institutional investors are considering adopting, or have already adopted, some form of sustainable investing like ESG integration in their portfolios.

As sustainable investors pay more attention to ESG data, so do corporations that need those investors. Data used by sustainable investors now play a prominent role in business plans for most publicly traded companies. As evidence, MSCI, a leading provider of sustainability data, rates more than 8,500 companies and over 680,000 equity and fixed-income securities throughout the world (MSCI, 2020). A slight change in a company's sustainability rating might distinguish whether large investment firms like BlackRock continue to hold the stock.

In other words, demand for sustainable investing data has increased rapidly since serious monitoring started in the early 1990s. As a result, the data and tools available for sustainable investors are quickly evolving with ever-increasing standards, protocols, and frameworks to match this demand. Many ESG data providers focus almost exclusively on sustainability and offer their services to help sustainable investors navigate the growing volume of information. Some of these research firms aggregate publicly available data like Refinitiv. However, most use objective and subjective data, like MSCI, ISS, Vigeo Eiris, TruValue Labs, Sustainalytics, and RepRisk. In addition, these firms specialize in processing ESG ratings and other information in a way that accurately assesses the sustainability profile for specific companies, funds, and portfolios.

Many data providers are even more specialized. For example, some provide data on specific ESG issues like gender equality data from Equileap or environmental data from the Carbon Disclosure Project (CDP). Sustainable investors also have many convenient apps to help them invest, such as Betterment, M1 Finance, Personal Capital, Open Invest, SoFi Invest, Ellevest, and Axos Invest. Even large financial services firms like Bloomberg now provide sustainability data. The next chapter discusses two highly rated online platforms—Personal Capital and Morningstar—along with an excellent software offering from Quicken Premier.

What are the concerns about the performance data for sustainable investing?[1]

With so many options for ESG data, sustainable investors express concern about inconsistency in the data. For instance, discrepancies exist in the number of providers. The Global Initiative for Sustainability Ratings identified 125 ESG data providers in 2016. Yet, Li and Polychronopoulos (2020) claimed that only 70 firms offer some form of ESG ratings. Confusion also exists about data providers due to the numerous name changes from partnerships, mergers, and acquisitions for data providers. For example, one of the best-known ESG data and analytics providers is the Institutional Shareholder Services (ISS). In 2020, Deutsche Boerse, the German stock exchange operator, purchased an 80% stake in ISS for $1.8 billion. ISS officially remains autonomous. As strange as this union may seem, this isn't the only time a stock exchange has invested in an ESG data provider. In 2021, the London Stock Exchange invested $27 billion to purchase Refinitiv, 45% owned by Thomson Reuters.

Another concern is that a growing strand of research questions the robustness and information value of ESG data (Cohen, Gurun, and Nguyen, 2021). As evidence, Li and Polychronopoulos (2020) showed that different processes for ESG rating providers can lead to the same company being ranked high by one provider and low by another. Some of the more prominent examples include Boeing, UnitedHealth Group, Walmart, and Wells Fargo. As further evidence, Li and Polychronopoulos used identical processes to construct sustainable investment portfolios. The only exception is that they used ESG data from two different well-known data providers. Over eight years, the portfolios provided considerable performance discrepancies. When using stocks from Europe, the ESG portfolios had an annual performance dispersion of 0.70 percentage points (9.4% vs. 8.7%), which amassed into a 10.0% cumulative difference over the entire period. Using U.S. stocks, the ESG performance dispersion increased to 1.30 percentage points a year (14.2% vs. 12.9%), and the overall performance discrepancy jumped up to 24.1% over eight years. In other words, the ESG provider picked by a sustainable investor can make a big difference. Sustainable investors need to make sure they do their homework so that they construct appropriate portfolios. The metrics and evaluation process used by their data provider should be consistent with their ESG preferences.

For now, sustainable investors must live with the good and the bad. Fortunately, many improvements have occurred in collecting ESG data. However, with so many choices for data providers and the confusion about rating accuracy, many institutional investors still believe that they lack adequate data sources and efficient tools to measure and track sustainable investment products. For example, a Morgan Stanley (2020a) survey highlighted that 29% of institutional investors list the quality of sustainability data as their top challenge, followed closely by 25%, stating that their biggest concern involved proof of financial performance. So, the two biggest complaints about sustainability investing from institutional investors are data issues. As for tools, 31% of institutional investors report that they didn't have adequate tools to assess sustainability properly within their portfolios. Thus, improving both data and tools available for investors are two ways to lower entry barriers into the sustainable investing industry.

> "Unfortunately, the lack of robust data by which ESG ratings are determined is a significant barrier to greater adoption of ESG strategies."
>
> —Feifei Li and Ari Polychronopoulos

What is the total number of sustainable investment funds?

One issue with tracking the performance of sustainable funds is the difficulty of identifying all sustainable investment funds. For instance, many challenges exist in counting all investment funds, like mutual funds, exchange-traded funds (ETFs), and variable annuity funds, with sustainability criteria in their investment process. As of 2020, the US SIF Foundation recognizes 836 registered sustainable investment firms housing 718 sustainable mutual funds and 94 sustainable ETFs. The US SIF Foundation also recognizes 905 alternative sustainable funds, including hedge funds, private equity funds, venture capital funds, and real estate funds like real estate investment trusts (REITs). Expanding this number even further could occur by including the rapidly growing impact investing sector. This sector focuses on more localized investment opportunities and products like low-interest loans and venture funds, typically offered through credit unions, community development banks, and specific charitable foundations (SIF, 2020). However, Morningstar can help narrow this list. As of 2020, when screening out funds that only "consider" sustainability criteria, Morningstar identified 358 sustainable mutual funds across various categories and asset classes.

Have sustainable investment funds outperformed traditional funds?

The most recent research suggests some outperformance for sustainable investment funds. Iachini (2020) ranked the performance of Morningstar's 358 sustainable mutual funds to other funds in the same relative Morningstar category between 2010 and 2020. The results showed that sustainable funds consistently rank around the middle of their peer group. In addition, when comparing the risk of sustainable funds to their traditional counterparts, Iachini found that sustainable funds have slightly lower standard deviations over 1-year, 3-year, 5-year, and 10-year periods, suggesting lower total risk.

Finally, Iachini analyzed 10 fund categories within three asset classes (U.S. equity, international equity, and bonds) during six major market corrections between 2009 and 2020. The results demonstrate that sustainable funds more frequently outperform their peer groups than underperform during these market downturns. For example, during the 2009 housing crisis and the 2020 COVID-19 pandemic, sustainable funds outperformed in almost all 10 categories. Moreover, they didn't underperform by more than half a percent in any category. Lins, Servaes, and Tamayo (2017) further supported these findings. In particular, the authors showed that high-rated sustainable stocks outperformed low-rated stocks by 4 to 7 percentage points during the 2009 housing crisis.

Sustainable investors should realize that these results don't suggest that sustainable funds guarantee a positive return during market corrections. On the contrary, most funds, including sustainable funds, typically lose value during market corrections. Nonetheless, in most categories during these specific downturns, sustainable funds lost less value than the other funds in their respective peer groups.

Several other recent studies find similar outperformance for sustainable funds or positive benefits for investing in firms with high ESG ratings (Clark, Feiner, and Viehs, 2015; Fulton, Kahn, and Sharples, 2012; Morningstar, 2021; Whelan, Atz, Hold, and Clark, 2020). For example, Clark et al. (2015) reported that most research shows that good sustainability standards can lower firms' cost of capital (90%), improve firms' operational performance (88%), and increase firms' stock price (80%). Moreover, many of these studies, like Whelan et al. (2020), highlighted a link between sustainable investing and

1. downside protection, especially during a social or economic crisis,
2. improved financial performance becoming more apparent over longer time horizons, and

3. outperformance, mainly limited to funds focusing on ESG integration instead of negative screening.

In-house research from Morgan Stanley also shows outperformance for sustainable funds. Morgan Stanley (2019) analyzed 10,723 mutual funds between 2004 and 2018 to compare the performance of sustainable funds to traditional funds. Its findings show no statistically significant difference between sustainable and traditional funds. However, like Iachini (2020), Morgan Stanley noted that sustainable funds might offer less volatility, suggesting potential market risk mitigation. Morgan Stanley (2020b, 2020c) provided evidence that sustainable funds had higher 2019 median returns for both U.S. equity funds (2.8 percentage points higher) and U.S. taxable bond funds (0.8 percentage points higher) than traditional funds in their peer group. One explanation for the performance gap in sustainable equity funds may be that these funds held more large-cap stocks and growth stocks.

Morgan Stanley also clearly shows that sustainable funds continued their outperformance in 2020 during the COVID-19 pandemic. For example, U.S. sustainable equity funds outperformed similar traditional equity funds in terms of total median return (4.3 percentage points higher) and median *downside deviation* (3.1 percentage points lower). Downside deviation measures downside risk based on the extent to which historical returns are lower than an investor's minimum acceptable return (MAR). Moreover, most of this outperformance occurred during the first half of 2020, when the median returns show a much larger downturn for traditional equity funds (–8.7%) than sustainable equity funds (–4.8%). This evidence suggests that sustainable funds did a better job managing risk.

Interestingly, the U.S. sustainable and traditional equity funds had similar rallies in the second half of 2020, with both increasing their median returns by more than 23%. As for bonds, a similar but smaller pattern occurred in 2020, with

U.S. sustainable bond funds also outperforming similar U.S. traditional bond funds in both total median return (0.9 percentage points higher) and median downside deviation (0.4 percentage points lower). In short, this evidence indicates that U.S. sustainable funds continued their 2019 outperformance of their traditional counterparts through the 2020 pandemic. Moreover, sustainable funds also performed remarkably better during the market downturn in the first half of 2020.

How has the performance of sustainable funds changed over time?

Overall, research on the performance of sustainable funds has been relatively consistent. For example, most earlier studies, primarily involving the United States, find no statistically significant difference between the risk-adjusted returns of sustainable funds and traditional funds (Bauer, Koedijk, and Otten, 2005; Guerard, 1997; Hamilton, Jo, and Statman, 1993; Kreander, Gray, Power, and Sinclair, 2005; Renneboog, Ter Horst, and Zhang, 2008a; Schröder, 2004; Statman, 2000, 2006). However, earlier studies report less outperformance than more recent ones.

A few earlier studies suggest a small upside for sustainable funds, primarily outside of the United States (Kreander, Gray, Power, and Sinclair, 2002; Orlitzky, Schmidt, and Rynes, 2003). However, many of these studies acknowledge inappropriate benchmarks, size bias, and time-varying results, potentially mitigating any outperformance. For example, in an Australian study, Bauer, Otten, and Rad (2006) showed that sustainable funds underperformed between 1992 and 1996. They underwent a catchup phase with more traditional funds but matched traditional funds more closely between 1996 and 2003.

Several early Asian studies find evidence of underperformance and suggest that sustainable investors pay an additional cost for investing in sustainable funds (Jin, Mitchell, and Piggott, 2006; Renneboog, Ter Horst, and Zhang, 2008b). Nonetheless, research generally concludes that sustainable investors don't have to sacrifice financial return to achieve a social return. Furthermore, more recent research suggests that sustainable funds may receive a slightly higher return than traditional funds. These findings appear robust, especially considering that the studies use diverse testing methods to measure the performance of sustainable funds in various countries and over different periods.

What are the performance implications of sustainable investment indices?

Analyzing sustainable investment indices can provide a clearer perspective on performance than sustainable investment funds. This additional transparency is because indices eliminate many common distortions and variations in actively managed investment funds, such as transaction costs, timing issues, and management skills. For example, the Domini 400 Social Index (DSI) was the first index to measure the performance of a broad universe of sustainable stocks in the United States. From its inception in May 1990 through March 1999, the DSI outperformed the S&P 500 by a cumulative difference of 81%. Interestingly, nearly two-thirds of the stocks in the DSI index were also in the S&P 500. In other words, the DSI eliminated about half of the S&P companies using negative screens for companies associated with sin industries like alcohol, tobacco, and gambling. The DSI added the other 143 companies using positive screens for 103 larger-cap companies with better industry representation and 40 smaller-cap companies with high rankings in product quality, corporate citizenship, and diversity issues. The DSI's makeup is relevant because most research attributes its outperformance to size bias, investment style, or industry exposure. In other words, the DSI negatively screened out larger-cap stocks in value-oriented sectors in the S&P 500 and positively screened for smaller-cap stocks in growth-oriented sectors (Bauer, Koedijk, and Otten, 2005; DiBartolomeo and Kurtz, 1999).

The number of sustainable indices multiplied in the early 2000s, with Calvert, Dow Jones, and others adding their indices. However, compared to the S&P 500 Index, the performance of most sustainability indices lagged during the first decade of the 2000s for similar allocation reasons that the DSI had previously outperformed in the 1990s. In particular, the weighting of sustainable indices leaned toward technology (tech) companies during the tech bubble that separated the two decades (DiBartolomeo and Kurtz, 2011; Statman, 2006).

Today the DSI is known as the MSCI KLD 400 Social Index. Given this index's unique mix of investment styles, sector exposure, and stocks with different market capitalizations, perhaps a better benchmark than the S&P 500 Index is the MSCI USA IMI. The MSCI USA IMI measures the performance of the U.S. market's small-, mid-, and large-cap segments. Return data show a high correlation between the two MSCI indices. For example, since 1999, the MSCI KLD 400 Social Index (7.39%) and the MSCI USA IMI (7.96%) have had almost identical annualized returns (MSCI, 2021).

Research from other sustainable indices provides similar findings. For example, Kurtz and DiBartolomeo (2005) examined the performance of the KLD Catholics Value (CV) 400 Index. They found that CV investors don't have to sacrifice investment returns to follow their values. For a more comprehensive approach, Schröder (2004, 2007) compared benchmarks for 10 and 29 sustainable funds, respectively. He found that traditional indices don't outperform sustainable funds. However, Schröder noted that 20 of the 29 sustainable indices have higher risks relative to their benchmarks. Managi, Okimoto, and Matsuda (2012) also provided an extensive review of sustainable indices in the United States, the United Kingdom, and Japan. They confirmed that sustainable indices don't suffer from a performance disadvantage. Finally, O'Brien, Liao, and Campagna (2018) examined the leading sustainable equity indices over time and agreed with earlier studies. They found no statistically significant difference in return or risk profiles between sustainable indices and traditional market benchmarks.

One important caveat regarding these findings: an extended timeline is unavailable to measure performance for many newer sustainable indices. Currently, the overarching narrative is that little difference exists in long-term performance between sustainable indices and their benchmarks. Yet, the consensus may change as more research becomes available, especially using risk-adjusted performance data.

How fast is investor demand for sustainable investing growing?

Sustainable investing continues to be on a path for future growth. Overall, the total value of sustainable AUM in the United States grew 42% between 2018 and year-end 2019 to around $17.1 trillion. This amount represents approximately one out of every three dollars of the $51.4 trillion in total U.S. assets under professional management (SIF, 2020). Astonishingly, that growth rate was even higher the following year, nearly doubling between 2019 and 2020. Consistent with this momentum, investors designated about a third of all AUM toward sustainable investing strategies at the start of 2020.

Furthermore, both individual and institutional investors are quickly adopting sustainable investing strategies. From an individual investor perspective, roughly half of all U.S. individual investors in 2020 are sustainable investors. More impressive, from an organizational perspective, approximately four out of five U.S. institutional investors in 2020 currently incorporate sustainability criteria into their overall investment process (SIF, 2020). Additional research provides more context for the growth of sustainable investing among institutional investors. For example, EY (2020) reports that only about half (49%) of the 73 institutional investors surveyed already invest in ESG products. However, EY notes that nearly 9 out of 10 institutional investors (roughly 88%) asked how their managers incorporate ESG into the investment strategies within their portfolios. Another recent survey among institutional investors reports that 95% use or plan to use some form of sustainable investing within their portfolios. Moreover, looking forward, the majority (57%) of these respondents agree that they may only allocate funds sometime in the future to investors with a formal sustainable investment process (Morgan Stanley, 2020a).

As for requiring investors to have a sustainable investment process, some contend that the future is now. As evidence, the percentage of organizations required to invest in sustainable investment products almost doubled between 2019 (14%) and 2020 (26%). Organizations that were "not required but anticipated being required to invest in sustainable investment products with the next two years" also rose dramatically between 2019 (11%) and 2020 (19%). Thus, 45% of the organizations in 2020 must invest in sustainable investment products or expect such a requirement within the next two years. When we break down the 2020 numbers by region, we see that European organizations lead the way, with 42% currently required to invest in sustainable assets versus only 15% for North American organizations, and another 42% expect such a requirement within the next two years versus only 7% for North American organizations (EY, 2020).

From the wealth manager's perspective, the entire wealth management industry may need to make substantial adjustments to client portfolios and the overall investment process to account for the growth in sustainable investing. One issue in this industry is that some business lines, mainly passive, may need to be realigned to meet stringent sustainability requirements, particularly in Europe. In other words, an increase in wealth managers and other organizations divesting incompatible business lines with the organization's new sustainability goals is likely soon. Nearly half of wealth managers (49%) already agree that sustainability requirements profoundly affect their divestment strategies (Mize, Reilly, and Veissed, 2021).

Although inflows for sustainable investing set new records for 2018, 2019, and 2020, the magnitude of the growth is impressive. For around six years, inflows into sustainable funds slowly ticked up from less than $3 billion in 2013 to a previous calendar-year record of $5.4 billion in 2018. Inflows more than quadrupled to $21.4 billion through the end of 2019. Even more impressive, these record inflows continued for 2020, with inflows more than doubling to $51.1 billion to set a new record high—a record more than nine times higher than the record from just two years prior. In the fourth quarter of 2020 alone, inflows of $20.5 billion nearly equaled the entire amount of inflows for all of 2019. From a total market perspective, sustainable funds captured almost a quarter of all net inflows into the U.S. stock and bond mutual funds during 2020 (Hale, 2021; Morningstar, 2021; SIF, 2020; Stevens, 2019).

"Unquestionably we are seeing more demand worldwide. . . . I would say it is 90–10 in favor of what we are doing, and maybe it's 95–5."

—Larry Fink

Hale (2020) tracked the sustainable fund launches between 2005 and 2019 and identified a noticeable uptick in sustainable fund launches in 2015 (24 funds) compared to the average for the 10 prior years (8.7 funds). Moreover, the following four consecutive years would all see at least 30 new funds launched: 2016 (37), 2017 (44), 2018 (38), and 2019 (30). Much of the growth occurred by adding 106 passively managed sustainable funds, of which 77 were ETFs. ETFs represented 40% of total inflows for sustainable funds for 2019. Finally, Hale listed the four largest investors, accounting for most of the 2019 inflows for sustainable investing.

- BlackRock collected $5 billion with its 15 sustainable funds.
- Calvert added $3.7 billion within its 28 sustainable funds.
- Teacher's Insurance and Annuity Association (TIAA)/ Nuveen received $2.8 billion within its 16 sustainable funds.
- Vanguard obtained $2.7 billion within its 14 sustainable funds.

That growth occurred before the release of the 2020 numbers. Morningstar (2021) reports the launching of 71 sustainable funds in 2020, easily breaking the old record of 44 in 2017. In addition, the popularity of passive funds continues to grow. As evidence, 29 of the 71 new funds are ETFs, topping the previous highwater mark of 21 in 2016. Moreover, some of the other 42 open-end funds also employ ETFs within their underlying holdings, like the 11 LifePath ESG Index target-date funds (TDFs) added by BlackRock.

What factors are likely to affect the demand for sustainable investing going forward?

Sustainable funds attracted over $21 billion of inflows for the first quarter of 2021, roughly the same amount of inflows generated for all of 2019. Each new year seems to bring a new record. Yet, record growth is not mathematically sustainable forever, even for investing with sustainable in its name. Still, future investor demand should remain strong for several reasons. First, global issues like climate change may worsen, motivating more investors into the sustainable investment space.

Second, more companies and government employers continue to switch from defined benefit to defined contribution plans like 401(k) plans. Iacurci (2020) reported that sustainable funds make up only a fraction—about a tenth of 1%—of all 401(k) assets and that only 3% of 401(k) plans hold a sustainable fund. In short, few sustainable funds are in the 401(k) space, suggesting that this area is ripe for future growth. Moreover, the Biden administration is seeking to change the rules to enable businesses to offer sustainable funds to employees in retirement plans.

Third, demand should remain high, considering that younger generations are far more interested in sustainable

> "It's kind of amazing ESG assets have grown so much when they're basically limited to [being] outside of 401(k) plans."
>
> —Jon Hale

investing than older generations. Cerulli (2020) broke down demand for sustainable investing by each generation and showed high anticipated demand for

- 84% of Millennials,
- 34% of Generation X,
- 14% of Baby Boomers, and
- only 8% of the Silent and Greatest Generations.

Additionally, anticipated demand is likely high for 70% of Generation Z, suggesting that sustainable investing isn't a generational fad. Finally, Mirjam Staub-Bisang, Senior Advisor to BlackRock's Sustainability Investing Business, posits that as these younger generations become decision makers in the future, they are likely to favor stricter regulations to ensure companies act responsibly. Such action should incentivize companies to take ESG ratings even more seriously. Thus, strong demand for sustainable investment products should continue for the foreseeable future.

Besides growing inflows, increased adoption rates are likely to help drive future growth in sustainable investing. The institutional investors already adopting sustainability investing strategies increased 10 percentage points from 2017 (70%) to 2019 (80%). A survey of institutional investors by Morgan Stanley (2020a) reported that the four most prominent factors for the recent momentum toward sustainability investing are constituent demand (81%), financial return potential (78%), evolving policy and regulations (76%), and risk management (75%). Interestingly, when asked about their benefits for embracing sustainable investing, a much larger percentage of sustainable institutional

"The public—especially the increasing number of young people moving into leadership and decision-making positions—are attaching greater importance to how companies address their responsibilities. . . . Sustainability is the future of investing and can no longer be ignored."

—Mirjam Staub-Bisang

investors (63%) listed reputational benefits compared to the next three highest choices: improved stakeholder engagement (49%), enhanced ESG outcomes (43%), and enhanced financial performance (34%). These results suggest that reputational benefits and investor demand may have played a significant role in the recent meteoric rise of sustainability investing.

Has the growth in investor demand driven the recent outperformance in sustainable investing?

Some concerns exist that the growing market for sustainable equity funds may slow, affecting the recent outperformance. For example, Gantchev, Giannetti, and Li (2021) examined the ever-increasing demand for sustainable funds since the 2016 introduction of Morningstar's sustainability ratings, known as *globe ratings*. They showed that mutual funds attempt to improve their globe ratings by purchasing more sustainable stocks. They also contended that record demand put upward pressure on sustainable stock prices, making stocks with high sustainability ratings overvalued. They didn't necessarily predict a sustainable investing bubble, but they stressed that a trade-off occurred between improving sustainability scores and performance returns. These authors concluded that a new equilibrium would likely emerge once investors realized that sustainable stocks were overvalued and no longer traded to improve their globe ratings. In short, they suggested that these market inefficiency issues would be challenging to address as long as fund managers had incentives to compete for inflows based on two different and possibly conflicting dimensions, like sustainability scores versus financial performance.

Which of the three ESG criteria has historically performed better?

Sustainable investing is growing so fast that specific labels can have huge reputational effects. For instance, the primary force driving sustainable bonds is the demand for green

> "In our purportedly enlightened era, we pin scarlet letters on allegedly offending corporations without bothering much about facts and circumstances and seemingly without caring about the unwarranted harm such labeling can engender."
>
> —Hester Pierce

bonds (Morgan Stanley, 2020a). SEC Commissioner Hester Pierce compared E, S, and G labels to Nathaniel Hawthorne's *The Scarlet Letter*. Some debate exists about which of the three labels is most important. SIF (2020) stated that S has the biggest AUM, but E isn't far behind and has faster growth. This situation is probably due to the heightened concern around climate change.

That said, Fulton, Khan, and Sharples (2012) stated that G is the most important and most researched factor, with 20 studies focusing on G, 10 on E, and only 8 on S. They made several other key observations. First, 14 studies (8 for G, 5 for E, and 1 for S) find a positive correlation between higher ESG scores and a lower cost of capital. As for the correlation between higher ESG scores and higher market-based performance (higher returns),

- G had a positive correlation for seven of eight studies, with one neutral;
- E had a positive correlation for three of four studies, with one neutral; and
- S had a positive correlation for four of five studies, with one mixed.

In total, 14 of 17 studies found a market-based performance advantage (higher returns), with none classified as unfavorable.

Still, not all research agrees. Take E standards as an example. On the one hand, some studies documented performance advantages for stocks with higher E standards (Derwall, Guenster, Bauer, and Koedijk, 2005; Guenster, Bauer, Derwall, and Koedijk, 2011). On the other hand, other research provided evidence of outperformance for stocks of firms with higher total CO_2 emissions (including changes in emissions), suggesting a carbon premium (Bolton and Kacperczyk, 2021). Another study suggested that green assets have low expected returns because they hedged climate risk and investors enjoy holding them. This study also concluded that sustainable investing shifts investment toward green firms and makes firms greener (Pástor, Stambaugh, and Taylor, 2021).

As for governance (G), Gompers, Ishii, and Metrick (2001) examined 24 specific G standards for 1,500 U.S. companies during the 1990s and provided evidence of a direct relationship between higher G standards and higher performance. Interestingly, these authors also showed that companies with G policies favoring management over shareholders, like poison pill provisions, tend to have lower price-to-book ratios. A *poison pill* is a financial tactic or provision used by a company to make an unwanted takeover prohibitively expensive or less desirable. The authors concluded that firms can add value simply by eliminating just one G provision favoring management over shareholders and can experience substantial long-term benefits by eliminating several G provisions. This study was influential in paving the way forward for improved G standards.

Similarly, Ferrell, Hao, and Renneboog (2016) provided supporting evidence that well-governed firms with lower managerial entrenchment engage more in corporate social responsibility (CSR). *Managerial entrenchment* refers to the behavior that managers choose to maintain their positions and pursue their interests. Managers can entrench themselves by making manager-specific investments that make replacing them costly. Thus, managerial entrenchment can lead managers who abuse their power to further their interests at shareholders' expense. The authors establish that CSR positively affects value and mitigates the negative impact of managerial entrenchment on value.

Finally, Pedersen, Fitzgibbons, and Pomorski (2021) found that ESG portfolios are slightly less efficient than traditional portfolios. However, some sustainable preferences are more costly than others, such as specific S criteria like screening out sin stocks. Yet, the predicted impact on returns is positive for some specific G criteria and close to zero for both the specific E criteria (low carbon emissions) and commercial ESG measures.

What are the performance implications of sustainable investing when analyzing the fixed-income market?

Sustainable investing is attracting more interest among bond investors. Morgan Stanley (2020a) reports that the excitement around green bonds is currently driving sustainable bond funds. A *green bond* is a fixed-income instrument specifically earmarked to raise money for environmentally friendly projects. Green bond fund projects help the environment and can offer similar returns as traditional bonds. Green bonds have increased in popularity, especially in industries where the environment is a critical financial resource (Flammer, 2021). In 2020, the green bond market grew to over \$1 trillion, which is on par with the U.S. high-yield corporate debt market and could double during 2021. Sustainable bond investors should know that each green bond has different priorities. For example, for every \$1 invested in the Calvert Green Bond Fund (CGAFX), sustainable investors can expect 38 cents to go toward renewable energy, 22 cents toward green-building projects, and 8 cents toward low-carbon transportation (Huang, 2021).

The performance also varies among sustainable bond funds compared to a traditional benchmark like the Agg Index (Bloomberg Barclays US Aggregate Bond Index). For instance, looking at annualized returns between 2018 and 2020, the CGAFX lagged the Agg Index by 30 basis points. A *basis point* is a standard unit of measure for interest rates and other percentages in finance, equaling one-hundredth of a percent. On the other hand, the Brown Advisory Sustainable Bond Fund (BASBX) outperformed the Agg Index by 50 basis points over the same period (Huang, 2021).

Academic research also focuses on environmental issues in the sustainable bond market. For example, a recent study suggested that counties more versus less likely affected by climate change have higher issuance costs for long-term municipal bonds (Painter, 2020). Another study found that municipalities issue green bonds at a premium compared to more traditional municipal bonds (Baker, Bergstresser, Serafeim, and Wurgler, 2018). However, research typically suggests, if anything, a slight performance advantage for sustainable bonds (Barclays, 2016; Derwall and Koedijk, 2009; Larcker and Watts, 2019). For example, Derwall and Koedijk (2009) tracked sustainable bonds between 1987 and 2003 and found no underperformance compared to similar traditional bond funds (–1.08% vs. –1.28%, respectively). Moreover, the annualized returns for the sustainable balance funds holding stocks and fixed-income securities were over 1.36 percentage points higher than their matched traditional balanced funds (0.11% vs. –1.25%, respectively).

Being green can also improve the solvency of borrowing firms, especially involving default rates, credit spreads, and the cost of debt financing (Barth, Hübel, and Scholz, 2021; Bauer and Hann, 2014; Boubaker, Cellier, Manita, and Saeed, 2020; Chava, 2014; DiBartolomeo, 2010; Goss, 2007; Goss and Roberts, 2011). For instance, Goss (2007) examined 1,295 U.S. nonfinancial firms between 1991 and 2003. He found that firms in the bottom versus top sustainable quartile were more than twice as likely to default.

Bauer and Hann (2014) provided additional evidence that sustainable firms are less likely to experience financial distress. They analyzed the environmental profile of 582 U.S. public corporations between 1995 and 2006. Their evidence suggests that firms can lower their cost of debt and increase their credit rating by raising their environmental standards. Conversely, lower environmental standards can decrease the solvency of borrowing firms by increasing their exposure to costly regulatory, legal, and reputational risks.

Flammer (2021) went further regarding the efficacy of green bonds. He noted five specific positive attributes for green bond issuers:

- Positive announcement returns in the stock market, especially if the green bonds are certified and even more so for first-time issuers;
- Better operating performance and long-term value creation;
- Enhanced environmental performance, including higher environmental ratings and lower CO_2 emissions;
- More green innovations; and
- A higher percentage of long-term and environmentally sensitive investors.

What performance critiques or implications relate to screening?

"Win-win arguments promoting both bigger profits and better social returns are illogical. . . . Follow your values, but keep your eyes open."

—Robert Armstrong

The most documented financial performance critique for sustainable investing concerns negative screening (Adler and Kritzman, 2008; Geczy, Stambaugh, and Levin, 2005). When sustainable investors incorporate screens for specific ESG criteria, they are effectively shrinking the available investment universe. A smaller investment universe can theoretically decrease return by limiting investment opportunities and increase risk by limiting diversification. Thus, screening can be a poor recipe for maximizing risk-adjusted returns. Armstrong (2020) agrees and warns investors about the fallacy of sustainable investing. He contends that an uncompromising commitment to specific investment factors like ESG criteria can lead to long periods of underperformance and a painful experience for unsuspecting investors.

In response to these efficiency concerns, most sustainable investors concede that screening reduces opportunities for investment and diversification. Yet, the case for sustainable investing is that screening also reduces poor investments from the sustainable investment universe, offering arguably superior return and risk benefits. Simply put, some sustainable investors believe that screening can increase financial returns by eliminating firms not actively engaged in CSR. In addition, sustainability criteria like ESG factors can help identify specific firms' long-term opportunities and risks for these sustainable investors. Camejo (2002) agreed and stated that sustainable investors can use screens to reduce company-specific risk and liabilities and identify firms with better finances and more efficient management. On the other hand, Capelle-Blancard and Monjon (2014) suggested that greater screening intensity can slightly reduce financial performance, but the type of screening matters considerably. For example, screening out entire sectors or industries, which is common when avoiding sin stocks, is more detrimental to financial performance than screening that transverses all sectors such as best in class based on a principled rating system.

Do sin stocks outperform sustainable stocks?

Most research suggests that sin stocks outperform other stocks (Fabozzi, Ma, and Oliphant, 2008; Hong and Kacperczyk, 2009; Kim and Venkatachalam, 2011; Statman and Glushkov, 2009). For example, Hong and Kacperczyk (2009) found that sin stocks outpaced other stocks by roughly 2.5 percentage points annually between 1965 and 2006. Like similar studies, they suggested that the neglected firm effect partially explained this outperformance. The *neglected firm effect* is a financial theory that explains the tendency for certain lesser-known companies to outperform better-known companies. The authors showed that many investors and analysts avoid sin stocks, which receive about 21% less analyst coverage.

Fabozzi, Ma, and Oliphant (2008) found even more impressive results when analyzing 267 sin stocks between 1970 and 2007. They calculated that the average sin stock earned a 19%

return, and the average sin industry earned over 13%. Their evidence suggests that if investors want to maximize their financial returns, they should consider a fund like the Vice Fund (now known as the Vitium Global Fund), which invests heavily in sin stocks in the alcohol, tobacco, gaming, and defense industries. In its first 10 years following its inception in 2002, the VICE Fund provided an average annualized return of 8.88% compared to only 6.22% for the S&P 500 Index.

Sustainable investors need not worry too much that they are missing out on financial returns from sin stocks. First, although the VICE Fund continued to perform well through 2017, it declined 21% in 2018 compared to only a 4% decline for the S&P 500 Index, essentially erasing all of its previous outperformance since inception. Also, just because sin stocks have performed well in the past doesn't mean that sustainable stocks have performed poorly. Statman and Glushkov (2009) compared sin stocks, sustainable stocks, and traditional stocks. They found that both sin stocks and high-ranking sustainable stocks outperform traditional stocks. Setting moral contradictions aside, these results suggest that investing in sin stocks and high-ranking sustainable stocks might improve performance.

Finally, Lu and Balvers (2015) acknowledged that sin stocks earn abnormal returns. However, they contended that investors should expect these returns due to an additional risk factor—the boycott risk factor. The *boycott risk factor* demands that morally unconstrained investors receive a premium for incurring the additional risk of holding assets that other sustainable investors actively boycott. In other words, they found no risk-adjusted outperformance for sin stocks because the abnormal returns for sin stocks disappear once they are properly adjusted using a boycott risk factor.

Is sustainable investing ethical window dressing?

Sustainable investors want assurance that they aren't investing in a sin stock masquerading as a sustainable stock. Window dressing is a huge concern in sustainable investing. *Window dressing* refers to management actions to improve the appearance of a company's financial statements. Kempf and Osthoff (2008) tested whether sustainable funds are traditional funds

> "[Sustainable investing is] frequently a cloak for actions that are justified on other grounds rather than a reason for those actions."
> —Milton Friedman

in disguise by comparing their respective E and S standards between 1991 and 2004. The authors found no evidence of window-dressing strategies. Moreover, their evidence shows that sustainable funds have higher rankings than traditional funds based on every measured criterion. Still, as sustainable investing becomes more mainstream, other firms are likely to have incentives to improve their ESG ratings to appeal to sustainable investors. Further work on transparency is needed to assure that firms viewing ESG ratings as a game they can manipulate to their advantage aren't scamming sustainable investors. Sustainable investors should be mindful of ESG window-dressing strategies and make sure that they rely on research from multiple nonbiased sources.

How has sustainable investing had a positive benefit on changing society or corporate behavior?

Measuring the impact of sustainable investment on changing society or corporate behavior is challenging, especially given the various definitions and goals under the sustainable investing umbrella. The most promising avenue for societal change is likely to be through the 17 interlinked Sustainable Development Goals (SDGs) proposed in 2015 by the UN General Assembly and made more actionable through a 2017 UN Resolution. The resolution identified specific targets for each SDG and

> "It's easy to see parallels between the current divestment campaigns over climate change and guns, and the earlier campaign to divest from companies doing business with apartheid South Africa."
> —Cecelie Counts

provided indicators for reaching the targets. In addition, the UN provides an annual progress report on these goals. For example, UN (2020) not only provides an overview and a progress summary for SDG targets, but also contains a specific progress report for each SDG. Moreover, UN (2020) outlines the need for data innovations, mainly due to the impact of the COVID-19 pandemic.

Although the UN shows progress toward meeting some goals, progress in other areas has stalled or even reversed. In many ways, COVID-19 highlighted the need for the SDGs. Although COVID-19 has been a short-term deterrent for progress, it may be a long-term catalyst for advancement. Given that the proposed dates for meeting most targets are between 2020 and 2030, with no end date given for some targets, the true power of sustainable investing is likely to be more evident soon.

For now, the most famous historical victory for sustainable investing might be the perceived role that divestment played in ending the apartheid regime in South Africa. However, some contend that this role has been somewhat exaggerated. Cecelie Counts, a founding member of the Southern Africa Support Project, maintains that divestment played a part but was just one weapon in a long battle fought on various fronts. According to Counts (2013), the shareholder boycotts mostly informed South African leaders about the global opposition to their apartheid policies. Teoh, Welch, and Wazzan (1999) found no empirical support for the common perception that the antiapartheid divestiture adversely affected the South African financial sector. Nonetheless, perception is often reality. Even if the perceived benefits outweighed the practical ones, the perceived impact of the South African divestment served as a significant catalyst for the current sustainable investment movement.

Since the South African divestment, other divestments and boycotts in other countries have occurred, like the U.S.-led divestment of Sudan in 2007 and the ongoing Arab League's boycott of Israel. In addition, many large investment funds have publicly divested from several industries, including the tobacco, weapons, and fossil fuels industries. As for the latter, a rapidly growing list of institutions, including several well-known universities, has already divested fossil fuels. For example, Fossil Free (2021) claimed that 1,325 institutions and over 58,000 investors have begun or committed to divesting roughly $14.56 trillion in AUM.

Fossil fuel divestment is quickly evolving into one of the most prominent divestment movements in history. For instance, more than 40 faith groups in 14 countries agreed in 2020 to divest from fossil fuels. Even countries have started to join the list. In 2015, Norway divested away from coal in their Government Pension Fund Global (GPFG). In 2018, Ireland became the first country to sell off its investments in any fossil fuel companies. In 2019, Norway announced its intention to increase its commitment and divest from any fossil fuel companies lacking renewable energy divisions. Norway's divestment is especially remarkable given that the country used its large oil reserves to build the world's largest sovereign wealth fund, the GPFG, worth over $1 trillion as of 2021. A *sovereign wealth fund* is a state-owned investment fund with money generated by the government.

Big Oil has certainly noticed investor behavior and increased its efforts in the renewable energy space. *Big Oil* is a term used to describe the world's six or seven largest publicly traded oil and gas companies. Cohen, Gurun, and Nguyen (2021) analyzed green energy patents issued between 2008 and 2017. They found that Big Oil companies invested about three times more than the average firm in climate change-mitigation technology. Among the top 50 green patent innovators are several notable Big Oil companies with lower relative ESG scores, including Exxon Mobil (ranked #11), Royal Dutch Shell (#18), BP (#27), ConocoPhillips (#28), and Chevron (#30). The authors questioned whether current divestment strategies are optimal and proposed that reward-based incentives might lead to more efficient outcomes.

Similar but somewhat quieter calls exist for divestment from the tobacco and weapons industries. However, once again, research questions divestment's impact. Blitz and Swinkels (2020) suggested that divestment in the tobacco industry might be counterproductive regarding the change that many sustainable investors want to see in the industry. The authors proposed that investors in tobacco companies aren't financing the tobacco business because they aren't providing any new capital to tobacco firms for expanding their operations. On the contrary, sustainable investors sell their right to vote and initiate proposals at shareholder meetings, making it difficult to enact change toward more sustainable corporate behavior. The authors conclude that sustainable investors should consider differentiating their policies, depending on the external financing needs of companies in specific industries.

Davies and Van Wesep (2018) examined divestment's additional unintended consequences. They showed that divestment depresses share prices. However, if managers acquiesce to the sustainable investors' demands, they risk increasing short-term prices at the cost of long-term profits. Given that most managerial contracts reward long-term performance, the authors contended that divestment is, at best, ineffective, and at worst, may curtail long-term performance.

Even when firms acquiesce to stakeholders' demands, no guarantee exists that they can create socially responsible policies that will work. Well-intended policies can even backfire. In 2018, protesters gathered outside of a Starbucks in Philadelphia, where police arrested two black men for trespassing because they wanted to use the bathroom even though they hadn't purchased anything. A growing number of social media users accused Starbucks of racial profiling and urged customers to boycott Starbucks. Starbucks quickly responded with a policy change that

"Any customer is welcome to use Starbucks spaces, including our restrooms, cafes and patios, regardless of whether they make a purchase."

—Starbucks

anybody could sit in their stores or use their bathroom even if they didn't make a purchase.

Gurun, Nickerson, and Solomon (2020) examined the impact of this policy change using cellphone location data. They showed that Starbucks's policy change led to a 7% dip in customer attendance relative to nearby coffee shops. Furthermore, the remaining customers spent 4.1% less time per visit. These results suggest that noncustomers somewhat crowded out paying customers. Although public urination citations decreased near Starbucks locations, Starbucks's policy also clearly decreased its customer base. In short, sustainable investing can affect corporate behavior, but measuring that change is difficult. Although most sustainable investors can point to positive change, some efforts may be ineffective or even counterproductive.

Can sustainable investors have their cake and eat it too?

Existing trends point to sustainable investing growing in AUM and societal impact. As a result, sustainable investing is no longer a fringe investment category that companies can ignore. Instead, it's quickly becoming the rule instead of the exception. Cliff Robins, the founder of the $2.2 billion hedge fund Blue Harbour Group, believes that companies will care about their ESG scores because all major investors now care about sustainable investing, such as endowments, foundations, pension funds, and labor unions (Stevens, 2019). In other words, social and financial performance is likely to be even more integrated moving forward.

As institutional investors move more toward sustainable investing, their performance expectations also appear to be changing. For example, nearly half (45%) of institutional

> "The largest investors in the world, which control how stocks are ultimately valued, care about this . . . the biggest asset managers in the world have now awoken and said 'ESG matters to me,' and therefore it's going to matter to companies."
> —Cliff Robbins

investors view generating a social return as equally crucial as generating a financial return. Moreover, four out of five institutional investors believe that companies with better ESG practices may provide higher long-term returns (Morgan Stanley, 2020a).

Recent research suggests some outperformance for sustainable funds and perhaps some downside protection. The protection could be critical going forward, given the impact of the unforeseen and unprecedented 2020 COVID-19 pandemic. This pandemic created extraordinary health and economic challenges on a global level. The investment industry quickly adjusted to new conditions and navigated a landscape with limited information about the present and future. As a prime example of the impact, never in recorded history have most world economies voluntarily shut down. The shutdowns ranged in time, location, and magnitude, including sudden, sporadic, complete, partial, geographically focused, and even specific sector and industry shutdowns. Savvy investors are aware that sustainable funds outperformed and provided protection during this time of uncertainty. Hence, investors' appetites for sustainable investing are likely to continue to grow. Moreover, the COVID-19 pandemic exacerbated many global issues like wealth inequality that sustainable investing tries to address, providing an even better recipe for increased demand. Thus, as the evidence favoring sustainable investing continues to grow, so do investors' hunger pangs, and many sustainable investors are eager to have their cake and eat it too.

What online resources are available for researching more information on the performance of sustainable investments?

Some specific websites provide ongoing and relevant research about sustainable investments, including the industry's growth, integration, and performance.

- The Global Sustainable Investment Alliance (GSIA) is a partnership encompassing the world's seven largest sustainable investment membership organizations (http://www.gsi-alliance.org). The website provides additional links to each organization, containing a wealth of educational material and current statistics on the sustainable investment industry for a specific region (Asia, Europe, Australia, Canada, the UK, the United States, and the Netherlands). As an example, below are the two largest organizations:
    - o European Sustainable Investment Forum (Eurosif) (https://www.eurosif.org)
    - o US Forum for Sustainable and Responsible Investment (US SIF) (https://www.ussif.org).
- Universities like Columbia and New York University as well as other organizations like the CFA Institute and Nuveen (a subsidiary of TIAA) offer specific resources on sustainability. In addition, many professional investment and service firms provide information on sustainable investing and business practices, including Blackrock, Charles Schwab, Ernst & Young, Morgan Stanley, Morningstar, and UBS. Below are two websites offering such information:
    - o The CFA Institute (https://www.cfainstitute.org/en/research/esg-investing).
    - o Morgan Stanley's Institute for Sustainable Investing (https://www.morganstanley.com/ideas?filter=sustainability).

Takeaways

In conclusion, investors need more robust and consistent data to quantify the relative financial performance of sustainable investment products. Improving data quality is paramount for the continued trajectory of the sustainable investing industry. Sustainable investing also needs to show its increasing impact on society. Otherwise, investor interest might wane, especially if it comes at the cost of financial performance. If future research shows that sustainable investors must pay a premium, growth in sustainable investing may slow and even decline. However, if future research finds no significant difference in the performance of traditional and sustainable investment funds, then sustainable investing may continue to grow as a means of extracting a second value—a social value—at no cost. Finally, a third scenario is possible. Some sustainable investors claim that companies sharing specific sustainability goals can better manage people, resources, and risk. If sustainable investment funds can produce higher risk-adjusted returns than traditional investment funds, they are likely to grow and become the conventional investment funds of the future.

Here are some key takeaways for sustainable investors from this chapter.

- Review the methodologies of different ESG rating providers and understand how to evaluate their metrics so that you can select the provider whose ratings most closely align with the ESG criteria you care about the most.
- Remember that most research finds that sustainable funds and indices are competitive with similar traditional funds and indices. Thus, sustainable investors don't have to sacrifice financial performance to retain their values.
- Be aware that some research finds recent outperformance for sustainable funds and highlights that they may offer some downside protection.
- Recognize that screening is less costly when used to identify company-specific risks or best-in-class across all sectors.
- Be aware that screening is more costly when eliminating entire sectors or industries such as sin stocks.

- Be cautious if you suspect window-dressing by a firm or fund manager, and make sure you rely on research from multiple nonbiased sources.
- Read the UN's report each year on the progress of SDGs to gauge whether society is advancing toward goals you value and gain insight on the specific SDGs that you want to support in your future portfolio.

6

BUILDING A PORTFOLIO WITH A PURPOSE

HOW TO BENEFIT YOU AND SOCIETY

> Done well, improving existing investment processes
> through the integration of ESG can mitigate portfolio
> risks and unlock long-term opportunities.
> —Mark Wiseman and Tariq Fancy

Interest in sustainable investing has surged worldwide in recent years. Today, many investors place increasing attention
on stakeholders, not just shareholders. Traditional and sustainable investors have different goals. Traditional investors want
to achieve an expected level of return while minimizing risk.
Their goal is financial. By contrast, sustainable investors seek
both financial and nonfinancial returns. Sustainable investors
look at environmental, social, and governance (ESG) factors,
along with financial analysis. Because their goals differ,
how they achieve them also varies. Although the same asset
classes are generally available to both types of investors, all
investments within each class aren't necessarily sustainable.
Therefore, those interested in sustainable investing have fewer
choices within each asset class than traditional investors.
Fortunately, interest in sustainable investing is growing, as are
the options for such investing. Sustainable investors have various motivations for their interests. One values-based motive
involves aligning investments with specific values. Another is

potential risk/return enhancement. A third motive is to have a positive environmental or social impact, leading to a better and more sustainable world.

This chapter focuses on building a portfolio containing at least some sustainable investments. Depending on the investor, sustainable investments may represent a core part of a portfolio or a satellite component. However, before discussing how to build a sustainable portfolio, the chapter discusses various misconceptions surrounding sustainable investing. The chapter then highlights several portfolio topics, including asset allocation, diversification, and rebalancing. By the end of this chapter, you should understand how to build a portfolio with a purpose that extends beyond purely financial returns.

What are common misconceptions about sustainable investing?

Many false impressions surround sustainable investing. Building and maintaining a portfolio containing some sustainable investments require dispelling these myths. Below are some of the major fallacies about sustainable investing.

- *Sustainable investments are a distinct asset class.* Investors shouldn't view ESG-focused investments as an exclusive, narrowly defined class of investments. Instead of viewing sustainable investments as a separate asset class, investors should view them through a lens applied across traditional and alternative asset classes. Traditional investments include stocks (equities), fixed income (bonds), and cash equivalents, whereas alternative investments are other classes like private equity, venture capital, and real estate. Thus, sustainable strategies work across a spectrum of different asset classes.
- *Sustainable investing requires rejecting foundational concepts.* Sustainable investing doesn't replace traditional asset management theory but adds to it. It requires combining

traditional investment approaches with ESG insights to understand better how to create value. Sustainable investing recognizes that companies engaged in solving the world's biggest challenges can be in the best position to grow and increase value.

- *Sustainable investing is about excluding "sin" stocks.* "Avoid" strategies exclude specific companies or sectors violating the asset owner's values. Although avoiding "sin" stocks like alcohol, tobacco, and firearms is a common strategy, other approaches are available to investors besides exclusionary screening. "Advanced" strategies focus on increasing exposure to positive ESG characteristics by aligning capital with certain behaviors or targeting specific positive social or environmental outcomes. These inclusionary strategies, including ESG, thematic, and impact investing, attempt to provide an informed analysis of investment risks and opportunities.

- *Sustainable investing focuses mainly on environmental issues.* Climate change and other environmental issues like carbon emissions and clean and accessible water are relevant concerns of sustainable investing. These matters only relate to the E (environment) in ESG. Other investors express concern about the S (social) and G (governance) factors. Additionally, some interconnectedness exists among ESG factors.

- *Sustainable investing is a fad.* As discussed in Chapter 1, sustainable investing has been around for hundreds of years. Although it's now part of the mainstream, many investors and financial professionals have been slow to embrace sustainable investing strategies. Nonetheless, the increasing amount of sustainable funds flow in recent years dispels the notion that sustainable investing is a fad. Instead, sustainable investing may represent the future of investing.

"We must shift our thinking away from short-term gain toward long-term investment and sustainability, and always have the next generations in mind with every decision we make."

—Deb Haaland

- *Sustainable investing isn't for serious or sophisticated investors.* A common stereotype is that only younger investors like millennials and women are interested in sustainable investing. All types of investors—individuals and institutions—are concerned about the impact of their investments. They want to align their investments with their core values or mission. Sustainable investing has gone mainstream and attracted increasing interest among investors worldwide. The rising stakeholder demand for meaningful action gives institutions little choice but to get out in front of the growing wave. The progress made by many large institutions to integrate ESG factors into their investing reinforces the notion that many sustainable investors are serious and sophisticated. Their age or gender doesn't define sustainable investors.

- *Sustainable funds are both few and expensive, and they require a substantial minimum investment.* Although institutional investors account for most global ESG investments, the universe of sustainable funds available to retail (individual) investors is significant and rising. Thus, investors have sufficient choices to build a diversified portfolio of stocks and bonds. Initially, sustainable funds charged high fees. As the number of actively managed open-end funds (mutual funds) grew, their expense ratios became more evenly distributed than their peers. The explosive growth of passive sustainable funds, especially exchange-traded funds, pushed down fees and minimum investment requirements. Today, many low-cost sustainable funds with low initial investments are available.

- *Investors sacrifice returns by aligning their investments with their values.* In theory, using exclusionary screens to constrain the investment universe should negatively affect returns and increase portfolio risk. Numerous academic and

> "Sustainability can't be like some sort of a moral sacrifice or political dilemma or a philanthropical cause. It has to be a design challenge."
> —Bjarke Ingels

other studies examine whether sustainable investing strategies result in a performance penalty. However, not all sustainable investment strategies are alike. Not surprisingly, the empirical results differ due to different samples, strategies, testing methodologies, and study periods. Individual studies show negative, positive, and mixed or neutral results. Overall, the results suggest that sustainable investing doesn't compromise performance, resulting in low returns. Incorporating ESG assessment with traditional financial analysis can provide the opportunity to identify the risks and opportunities for an investment in a specific company, resulting in capturing above-market returns. Investors can do well by doing good.

- *All businesses touting socially responsible or sustainable practices observe them.* Companies often devote considerable effort and money to create a positive public image. However, this image could be more marketing spin than reality. A corporation announcing a commitment to clean energy or human rights doesn't necessarily mean it will follow through. Thus, look beyond the rhetoric to determine whether the image accurately portrays the company or is marketing hype.

Why should sustainable investors take a portfolio perspective?

Are you familiar with the saying, "Don't put all of your eggs in one basket?" Its origin dates to the 17th century from *Don Quixote*, a Spanish novel by Miguel de Cervantes. If you place all your eggs in one basket and drop the basket, you may lose most, if not all, of your eggs. A similar concept applies to investing. If you concentrate your money on a single investment, like a stock, and it experiences a loss, your entire portfolio suffers. Consequently, holding only one security or investment is risky compared to having a properly diversified portfolio.

An alternative to examining risk and return in isolation is taking a *portfolio perspective*, which involves analyzing the risk-return trade-off of the entire portfolio, not the individual assets in isolation. The *risk-return trade-off* states that the potential return rises with an increase in risk. Thus, investors associate low-risk levels with low potential returns and high-risk levels with high potential returns. Although a single asset or security could be highly risky, adding it to a portfolio whose returns are not highly correlated reduces portfolio risk. Each investment reacts somewhat differently to new information. Because most assets are likely to provide a return similar to their expected return, they typically offset those in the portfolio that perform poorly. Thus, when the returns on one investment "zig," others "zag." Although having a more diversified portfolio doesn't eliminate all risk, it does reduce the risk of all assets in the portfolio being affected in the same way. In summary, building a portfolio out of many unrelated (uncorrelated) investments produces reduced risk (volatility) and improves the risk-return trade-off. Consequently, investors who fail to take a portfolio perspective bear risk unrewarded with a greater expected return.

What steps are in the portfolio management process?

The *portfolio management process* is a series of integrated steps designed to create and manage a portfolio to meet an investor's objectives within specified constraints. Following these steps and subcomponents creates a portfolio that can capture opportunities, withstand uncertainties, and meet investor needs. This process is similar for all investors, but those interested in sustainable investing must also incorporate their desire to align investments with their values. That is, they have dual objectives—financial and nonfinancial. As Figure 6.1 shows, the portfolio management

"When it comes to investing, there is no such thing as a one-size-fits-all portfolio."

—Barry Ritholtz

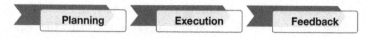

Figure 6.1 The Portfolio Management Process

process consists of three main steps: planning, execution, and feedback.

- **Planning**. This step involves several tasks.
  - o *Identify objectives and constraints*. Planning begins by evaluating your current situation relative to where you want to be—your investment goals and objectives. A portfolio should reflect what each investor intends to accomplish. Those interested in sustainable investing look beyond financial returns. This discovery process examines your values, beliefs, and priorities and centers on your risk-return profile within a set of constraints. *Investment constraints* are factors limiting investment options available to an investor. Constraints include your time horizon (i.e., when you need the money), liquidity and income needs, legal and regulatory situations, taxes, and any unique circumstances or preferences like your values. The analysis results in an investment policy statement (IPS) detailing an investor's investment objectives and constraints.
  - o *Determine your risk profile*. A risk profile evaluates of an individual's willingness and ability to take risks. It's crucial for determining a proper investment asset allocation for a portfolio because the potential return rises as risk increases. This principle is called the risk-return trade-off. The following link can help you determine your risk-return profile: http://www.iacr. com.au/files/docs/fna/fna%2014/fna%20part%20 3%20-%20risk%20profile.pdf.

o *Develop capital market expectations.* The next task is to form economic and capital market expectations to determine the risk and return of various asset classes over the long term. An asset class is a group of similar investment vehicles.

> "The difference between success and failure is not which stock you buy or which piece of real estate you buy, it's asset allocation."
>
> —Tony Robbins

o *Determine an asset allocation.* Next, you determine your *asset allocation,* which involves dividing an investment portfolio among various asset classes. Asset allocation tries to balance risk versus reward by adjusting each asset's percentage in an investment portfolio based on multiple factors discussed later in this chapter. Asset allocation and diversification remain the best ways to control portfolio risk during volatile markets.

o *Identify performance benchmarks.* The final task in the planning stage is to establish benchmarks for tracking a portfolio's performance. A *benchmark* is a standard against which you can measure a security, fund, or manager. Choosing a benchmark involves matching each of a portfolio's asset classes to an appropriate benchmark. For instance, if the portfolio consists of large-cap U.S. stocks, the Standards & Poor's (S&P) 500 index could serve as a proper benchmark. Such tracking enables you to adjust your portfolio over time.

• **Execution.** The second step in the portfolio management process is to execute the plan. It consists of two tasks.

o *Select investment options.* Having identified the appropriate asset classes, you need to identify the most attractive securities or funds within each asset class. This task largely rests on whether you prefer an active, passive, or hybrid investment strategy. A critical question that you should ask yourself is, "Should you be buying individual stocks?" Most sustainable investors should consider leaving investing in individual stocks and bonds to the professionals. Instead, they should invest in index funds, mutual funds, and exchange-traded funds (ETFs) specializing in sustainable investments. However, if you want to select individual stocks, you may want to consider free stock screeners, like those available from TD Ameritrade, Zacks, Google Finance, and FinViz.

- An *active investment* focuses on outperforming the market relative to a specific benchmark. Examples include focusing on a particular investment style like growth or value investing.

- A *passive investment* aims to replicate a particular benchmark or index to match its performance. Examples of passive strategies are *buy-and-hold*, which keeps a relatively stable portfolio over time despite short-term fluctuations, and indexing, which attempts to mimic a market index's performance. An active strategy responds more to changing expectations than a passive one. Thus, an active strategy tries to "beat the market" or index, but a passive strategy attempts to "meet the market" or benchmark by achieving similar returns. You may use either approach as an independent investor or use a portfolio manager to carry out a preferred investment strategy.

> "Don't look for the needle in the haystack. Just buy the haystack!"
>
> —*John Bogle*

- A *hybrid investment strategy* combines active and passive strategies.
   o *Construct a portfolio.* Once you select individual securities or funds, they should form a diversified portfolio whose characteristics align with your risk profile and values as a sustainable investor.

- **Feedback.** The final step involves several tasks.

  o *Monitor and rebalance.* You need to monitor your portfolio to determine whether the current weights differ

  > "The process of rebalancing an investment portfolio is completely dependent on the particular investor."
  > —Johanna Clayton

  from the targeted asset allocations due to market movements. If sufficient drift occurs, this could change the portfolio's risk exposure, requiring rebalancing to bring the portfolio back into alignment. For example, suppose you don't want the proportion of equities in your portfolio to exceed 50%. However, now it represents 60% of your portfolio due to increasing equity prices. As a result, you may decide to sell some stocks and buy securities in an underweighted asset class, say bonds. Before rebalancing, you should consider such factors as taxes and transaction costs. You may also need to modify your asset class weightings if you're not confident in your original strategy or if changes to your life merit altering your portfolio's asset allocation. *Rebalancing* is the process of realigning the weightings of a portfolio's assets. Portfolio rebalancing strategies are discussed further later in this chapter.

  o *Evaluate performance.* The final task is to measure your portfolio's performance relative to your expectations. Absolute return refers to an asset class's performance or strategy over a certain period without comparing it to any benchmark. By contrast, relative return is the difference between the absolute return and the market's or other similar investment's performance, gauged by a benchmark or index. Both absolute and relative measures are available and discussed later in this chapter.

What is an investment policy statement?

> "Similar to an expedition, an Investment Policy Statement (IPS) is a guide to your financial future."
>
> —Barbara A. Friedberg

An *investment policy statement* (IPS) is a document setting forth investment goals and objectives, strategies, and other issues that involve an investor's portfolio, including guidance for consistent, informed decision making. Thus, it provides a map or holistic review of the investment decision-making process. Financial advisors often use an IPS to document an investment plan with a client. If you work with an advisor, you should participate fully in this process and understand each step. Even if you don't work with an advisor, developing an IPS is a good exercise because doing so provides a framework for managing your portfolio. Think of it as an instruction manual for your investment activity.

Creating a good IPS with a financial advisor involves several steps. Some advisory firms have IPS software designed to capture financial advisors' and clients' information.

- **Meet with your financial advisor**. During this initial step, your advisor should provide an overview of the decision-making process used. Financial advisory firms typically have a version of an IPS. You should make sure that you understand this process and ask questions about any terms or issues you don't understand.
- **Specify your financial goals/objectives, values, and risk levels**. Next, you need to discuss who you are. You should explain why you're investing and indicate your quantitative and qualitative goals and objectives. For example, assume that your broad goal is long-term growth and capital appreciation. As a conservative investor, you expect to earn a long-term rate of return of 6% but are willing to accept a loss of up to 15% during any given year. If you're interested in sustainable investing, you need to articulate what ESG values are important.

You also need to articulate your risk and return parameters when investing. Often investors have conflicts between their willingness and ability to take risks in a portfolio. *Willingness* refers to the degree of investment risk an investor is comfortable taking. Your willingness to take risks depends on such factors as your personality type, investing experience, financial security, and inclination to think independently. Your ability to take risks depends primarily on your net worth or wealth relative to your debt. Other factors include your time horizon and expected income from investing. Moving through the IPS process should resolve any conflict between willingness and ability.

- **Set your asset allocation limits.** Whether you're a do-it-yourself (DIY) investor or working with a financial advisor, you need to establish a strategic portfolio allocation, which is critical in determining your portfolio's long-term performance. Deciding upon appropriate allocation parameters requires considering many factors like your goals and values, a required rate of return, acceptable risk levels, legal and liquidity requirements, taxes, time horizon, and unique circumstances.

  Historically, equities provide higher rates of return but with greater volatility than fixed-income investments. For example, a conservative investor may have a portfolio consisting of 55% in stocks, 40% in fixed income, and 5% in cash and cash equivalents. Within these asset classes, you should vary your holdings among different subclasses to achieve diversification benefits. For instance, you could break down your stock allocation into small/mid/large companies, growth and value styles, and your bond allocation by duration and quality. Duration has several meanings. *Duration* measures the time required, in years, for an investor to be repaid the bond's price by the bond's total cash flows. *Duration* is also a measure of the sensitivity of a bond's or fixed income portfolio's price to changes in interest rates. *Bond quality* is a bond's rating given by a rating service that indicates its credit quality. This rating considers a bond issuer's financial strength or ability to pay a bond's principal and interest.

- **Establish the procedures for running your portfolio.** This stage involves making such decisions as identifying screening criteria to select securities, determining monitoring procedures, how often to evaluate your portfolio, the benchmarks used, and rebalancing guidelines. It also sets forth the financial advisor's duties and responsibilities and associated fees and expenses.

- **Revisit your IPS periodically to make sure you're on track.** You shouldn't view your IPS as "set it and forget it." Instead, you should review it at least annually to ensure that you're moving toward achieving your investment goals and maintaining alignment between your investments and values. Also, you may have experienced changes in your circumstances that require revisiting your IPS.

Why should sustainable investors have an investment policy statement?

Having an IPS is helpful for several reasons. First, it offers guidance for making informed decisions, such as portfolio construction and a roadmap to successful investing. Second, it adheres to the fiduciary process. The law requires fiduciary advisors to act in their client's best interests. Third, an IPS helps maintain focus on your stated objectives and avoids deviations resulting from changing market conditions. For example, during periods of heightened market turbulence, a client may want to deviate from the IPS and make snap decisions due to emotions. Fourth, an IPS permits an advisor to point back to the plan and suggest that the client stick with it. Thus, it helps to impose investment discipline to stay the course with an investment strategy, ultimately leading to better outcomes. Finally, an IPS helps guard against mistakes and misdeeds when managing a portfolio. That is, it provides accountability.

What role does asset allocation play in the investment decision-making process?

Asset allocation is a critical step when making investment decisions. It's essential to help you reach your goals and reduce risk through diversification. More importantly, asset allocation accounts for most volatility and returns. Multiplying each asset's weight in the portfolio by its expected market return provides an average expected return. As a result, asset allocation is much more important than the investments you choose (security selection) and market timing in the investment decision-making process. Thus, it's perhaps the most critical aspect of your investing.

What types or classes of assets are available to sustainable investors?

Investments consist of two broad categories: traditional and alternative investments. Within each category are several asset classes. An *asset class* is a group of similar investments regarding financial characteristics and market behavior.

- **Traditional investments.** *Traditional investments* include publicly traded stocks (equities), bonds and fixed-income securities, and cash and cash equivalents, such as Treasury bills and notes, commercial paper, certificates of deposit (CDs), and money market funds. Historically, stock offered the highest risks and returns, followed by bonds, and cash and cash equivalents. Further dividing each asset class is also possible. For example, some ways to break down equities into subcategories include growth and value, location (domestic and foreign), and

> "Every portfolio benefits from bonds; they provide a cushion when the stock market hits a rough patch. But avoiding stocks completely could mean your investment won't grow any faster than the rate of inflation."
>
> —Suze Orman

market capitalization (small-cap, medium-cap, and large-cap). Growth investors seek companies that offer strong earnings growth, while value investors seek stocks that appear undervalued in the market. Small-cap stocks tend to be riskier than large-cap stocks. Although sustainable investments are available for virtually all asset classes, individuals interested in sustainable investing concentrate on traditional investments.

• **Alternative investments.** All other investments are *alternative investments*, like hedge funds, private equity, real estate, commodities, and infrastructure. These investments offer the potential of higher risk but with higher expected returns. In general, alternative investments are more complex and more opaque, require higher minimum investments and fees, and are less liquid and regulated. Consequently, sophisticated institutional investors like pension and endowment funds are the leading players in sustainable alternative investments. Alternative investments like hedge funds and private equity are unavailable to ordinary investors due to restrictions on the types of investors comprising a fund's investor pool. Historically, these investments catered to institutions and high net-worth individuals, not average retail investors. Today, alternative investments aren't just for the rich. Everyday investors with ordinary account balances can access many alternative asset classes.

Some alternative asset classes attract far less interest in sustainable investing than others. According to survey evidence, most hedge fund managers currently avoid sustainable investing. Why? An ESG hedge fund seems self-contradictory because the goals of absolute returns of hedge funds and sustainable investing ideals appear to be in opposition. Yet, ESG hedge funds are evolving as some hedge fund investors push for ESG-focused offerings, making saying "no" more difficult. Thus, if hedge fund managers believe that ESG investing is a way to make money, they may employ ESG strategies even if they don't necessarily share the values.

What are the main determinants of asset allocation?

Dividing an investment portfolio among various asset classes to reduce investment risk isn't a simple process. It involves multiple, interrelated factors, which change as an investor moves from one life stage to another. Figure 6.2 shows some main factors to consider in developing an asset allocation plan.

- **Goals**. Sustainable investors have both financial and nonfinancial goals that influence their asset allocation. Thus, different goals affect how a person invests and the risks an investor is willing to take.
- **Risk tolerance**. *Risk tolerance* refers to how much you're willing and able to lose of the original investment to get a higher future return. It's the lower between your willingness and ability to take risks. Determining your risk tolerance involves examining such factors as your investment goals and experience, time horizon, other financial resources, and "fear factor." If you're unsure how to do

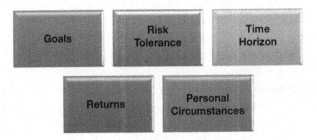

Figure 6.2 The Main Determinants of Asset Allocation

> "The single greatest edge an investor can have is a long-term orientation."
>
> —Seth Klarman

this, you can consult a financial advisor or use an online questionnaire (https://njaes.rutgers.edu/money/assessment-tools/investment-risk-tolerance-quiz.pdf) and calculator (https://www.calcxml.com/calculators/inv01).

Risk tolerance ranges from highly conservative to highly aggressive. The higher your risk tolerance, the more aggressive you can be by putting more funds in risky assets. Conservative approaches allocate additional funds to less risky and more liquid investments: cash equivalents, such as Treasury securities and insured certificates of deposit (CDs) and high-grade corporate and municipal bonds. Moderate approaches include such assets as high-grade preferred stock, convertible securities, and common stock, in addition to balanced and growth mutual funds. Finally, aggressive approaches allocate additional funds to investments with an increased risk of loss of principal and often more illiquidity, including alternative investments like hedge funds, private equity, and real estate, as well as speculative stocks and bonds. An objective of these increasingly risky approaches is to achieve higher expected returns.

- **Time horizon**. *Time horizon* is the amount of time available to achieve specific goals. The amount of time needed to reach your goal also drives asset allocation. For instance, someone saving for retirement can take more risk due to a longer time horizon. By contrast, if the goal is to have sufficient funds for a down payment on a house within the next five years, an investor should focus on less risky investments.
- **Returns.** Your return needs also influence your asset allocation decisions. To achieve higher returns, you need to invest in riskier assets. As already mentioned, stocks usually provide higher returns than bonds and cash over time but more volatility.

- **Personal circumstances**. These circumstances involve age, income, expenses including taxes, and assets and liabilities. Let's focus on age. If you're a young investor, you can generally afford to be more aggressive and invest more of your portfolio in risky assets like equities and less in fixed income to build long-term wealth. As you grow older, your allocation will likely shift to more conservative investments to generate income and preserve capital, especially as you approach retirement.

What are the two most common strategies for asset allocation and their advantages and disadvantages?

Figure 6.3 shows asset allocation strategies. Among the various asset allocation strategies available, age-based asset allocation and life-cycle asset allocation tend to be more common.

- **Age-based asset allocation**. As its name implies, age-based asset allocation depends on an investor's age. An old rule of thumb was that individuals should hold a percentage of stocks equal to 100 minus their age. Thus, for a typical 40-year-old, 60% of the portfolio should be equities, with the remaining proportion in debt and cash. This simple guideline applies to individuals investing in traditional investments. An underlying assumption is that younger investors can be more aggressive and hold more of their portfolios in stocks because they can weather the volatility of owning stocks over a time horizon. As they age, their portfolio mix becomes more

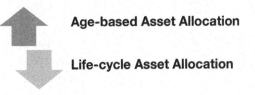

Age-based Asset Allocation

Life-cycle Asset Allocation

Figure 6.3 Two Main Asset Allocation Strategies

conservative as the balance gradually shifts as the percentage of stocks decreases with a corresponding increase in bonds.

o *Advantages*. One strength of this approach is its simplicity. You also aren't placing all your investments in a single asset class. Instead, each asset class behaves differently over time and has a different level of risk and return associated with it.

o *Disadvantages*. Not surprisingly, this modest guideline has limitations. For example, it ignores personal circumstances and applies to the "average" investor. Some financial professionals suggest using a base value of 110 or 120, depending on an investor's life expectancy or risk appetite to reduce these limitations. The higher the life expectancy or risk appetite, the higher the portion allocated to stocks. Thus, an investor with medium-risk tolerance would use a base value of 110, while someone with high-risk tolerance would use 120 as the base value. For example, suppose a 45-year-old investor has a medium-risk appetite. Subtracting that investor's age of 45 from 110 suggests investing 65% of that investor's portfolio in stocks with the remaining portion 35% in bonds.

o **Life-cycle asset allocation**. In life-cycle or target-date allocation, investors maximize their return on investment (ROI) based on factors such as their age, investment goals, and risk tolerance. Designing a standard allocation is complex because every investor has unique differences across these factors. Nonetheless, investors avoid the hassles involved in developing an asset allocation by using an *asset allocation fund*, providing them with a diversified portfolio of investments across different asset classes.

"Target-date funds have been nothing short of the biggest positive development for investors since the index fund."

—Christine Benz

One type of asset allocation fund is a life-cycle or target-date fund (TDF). A *TDF* is an investment vehicle whose asset allocation mix gets more conservative as the target date approaches. That is, a portfolio's composition gradually shifts from higher-risk stocks to lower-risk bonds and cash equivalents. A *target date* is when an investor plans to retire or start withdrawing funds. A TDF is typically a *fund of funds* (FoF), a vehicle investing in other mutual funds or exchange-traded funds (ETFs). TDFs are often the "default investment" for individual investors through defined contribution plans such as a 401(k). A *defined contribution plan* is a retirement plan where the employer, employee, or both regularly contribute.

TDFs have both advantages and disadvantages.

o *Advantages.* TDFs provide investors with a simple, convenient, and professionally managed way to save for retirement with low minimum investment and maintenance. They offer something for everyone, including active management, passive management, exposure to different markets, and a selection of asset allocation options. TDFs can broadly diversify across and within asset classes, offering an age-appropriate allocation due to continual portfolio rebalancing. The funds follow a *glide path*, a planned progression of asset allocation changes over time to reflect investors' changing tolerance for risk. Some TDFs use funds from other families, ETFs, or other types of holdings to increase diversification. Thus, this simple solution to asset allocation provides a diversified portfolio and an autopilot way to invest to avoid missteps.

o *Disadvantages.* TDFs provide a standardized solution for allocating portfolio assets, which is problematic because individual investors require individual solutions. This "one-size-fits-all" approach can't accommodate an individual's changing goals and needs or consider other investments or sources of income. Therefore, investors should periodically reevaluate a TDF to see if it's appropriate for their current situation. TDFs can also be expensive and involve high fees and expenses. Not all funds are created equal. For example, TDFs with the same target date, say 2045, may have different asset allocations, allocation glide paths, and investment styles. They also don't guarantee income and may not provide a sufficient inflation hedge. TDFs may lack diversification if they invest only in funds from the same fund family as Vanguard, Fidelity, and T. Rowe Prices. Investors buying TDFs outside an individual retirement account (IRA) or a qualified plan will likely realize capital gains triggering capital gains taxes. Finally, sustainable TDFs are relatively new. Consequently, they may be unable to reflect everyone's values involving sustainable investing.

In summary, this "one-size-fits-all" solution to asset allocation can be a reasonable option for average investors who are uncomfortable allocating their investments. Such investors may lack the time or expertise to build, monitor, and revise a diversified portfolio.

How do strategic asset allocation and tactical asset allocation differ, and what are the advantages and disadvantages of each?

Strategic asset allocation (SAA) and tactical asset allocation (TAA) have fundamental differences. SAA is fundamentally passive; tactical investing is fundamentally active. SAA is about time in the market, while tactical investing is about timing the market. The ideal asset allocation is the mix of investments earning the total return over time that you need.

- *Strategic asset allocation (SAA).* SAA sets long-term weights of the target asset classes based on the, expected rates of return for each asset class to achieve an investor's investment goals. For example, the SSA could consist of 10% cash, 50% stocks composed of 40% large-cap stocks and 10% small-cap stocks, 35% bonds, and 5% real estate. However, SAA isn't wholly "set-it-and-forget-it." Market fluctuations alter the percentage of each asset class in the portfolio, requiring rebalancing periodically to restore the desired long-term asset position. Investors can also adjust the fixed weight of the asset classes if circumstances merit, such as from changing investor circumstances, and then stick to the revised allocation.

    o *Advantages.* SAA focuses on constructing an *efficient portfolio* representing the optimal mix between different asset classes that maximize returns for a given risk level. It requires little effort to maintain, is tailored to an individual investor's profile, and limits taxes and trading costs. This relatively static or buy-and-hold investment strategy keeps investors from being sidetracked by making short-term emotional decisions. It relies on diversification to reduce risk and improve returns, thus taking advantage of market efficiency. Thus, SAA is an appropriate option for hands-off or risk-averse investors with a long-term time horizon. In addition, this strategy appeals to those with limited investing experience

> "Stock market goes up or down, and you can't adjust your portfolio based on the whims of the market, so you have to have a strategy in a position and stay true to that strategy and not pay attention to noise that could surround any particular investment."
>
> —John Paulson

who want to avoid constantly monitoring markets and their portfolios and being influenced by market trends or fads.

o *Disadvantages.* SAA focuses on an investor's profile but ignores noninvestor factors such as market opportunities. SAA can be effective, but it requires that investors maintain the discipline to follow the process. For example, the rebalancing process seems counterintuitive. It involves selling winners and buying the laggards to facilitate alignment with strategic allocation targets. Investors are often hesitant to sell a winner that's still promising or buy an asset that will continue to decline. Although this process involves "buying low and selling high," ask yourself the question, "Would I buy the asset today?" regardless of what you did in the past. If your response is yes, consider keeping it.

- *Tactical asset allocation (TAA).* TAA refers to a short-term change in the portfolio strategy resulting from changing expectations about entire markets or sectors and perceived mispricing opportunities. It tries to predict underlying shifts in market fundamentals, opportunities, or risks and take advantage of investment opportunities appearing in the marketplace. Thus, a tactical investor focuses on the present and near future and actively adjusts portfolio weightings to take advantage of external factors. TAA aims to increase risk-adjusted returns as compared to SAA.

  Tactical shifts can occur both between and within asset classes. For example, if commodities look attractive in the short run, an investor could shift 5% from cash and place it in commodities. Likewise, suppose the outlook for small-cap stocks appears favorable relative to large-cap stocks. In that case, a tactical decision could shift the allocation within stocks from 40%

to 30% large-cap and from 10% to 20% small-cap for a short period until conditions change. Tactical shifts are typically between 5% and 10% but can be lower.

o *Advantages.* TAA is a more flexible approach than SAA and offers the potential to increase returns, but it presents higher risks. Investors can use TAA techniques to beat the market by riding market trends. For example, this strategy may enable them to create additional value by changing a portfolio's original asset mix to take advantage of certain situations in the marketplace. Adopting this moderately active strategy requires recognizing when short- or medium-term opportunities end and then rebalancing the portfolio to return to its long-term weights.

o *Disadvantages.* TAA's chief drawback is that it's a form of market timing. An investor moves in and out of the market. Over the short run, returns are more random compared to the long term. Market-timing tactics generally cause more harm than good. Why? An investor's tactical investment decisions must be more often right than wrong to generate superior risk-adjusted returns and cover taxes and trading costs. In practice, this approach is exceedingly difficult to do well. Although market timing may seem appealing for those who can tolerate more risk, you should avoid it because you face a stacked deck against you for being successful.

In summary, some debate exists about each strategy. However, you don't necessarily have to choose one or the other. Both approaches can play a role in your overall strategy. Nonetheless, the current financial culture most commonly promotes SAA, especially for new or inexperienced investors with a long-term focus.

What are other types of asset allocation strategies?

Figure 6.4 shows other asset allocation strategies available to investors beyond SAA and TAA.

- *Constant-weighting asset allocation.* This approach continually rebalances a portfolio based on what happens in the market. An investor following this approach doesn't wait an extended period before rebalancing. Instead, the investor buys more of an asset that declines in price to take advantage of a price dip and sells an asset that increases in price to preserve a price gain.
- *Dynamic asset allocation.* This type of asset allocation constantly adjusts the asset mix based on the behavior of the market, specific securities, and the economy. It relies

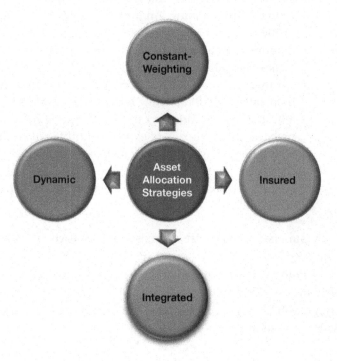

Figure 6.4 Other Asset Allocation Strategies beyond SAA and TAA

more on an investor's judgment in responding to the market changes than on a targeted asset mix. With this strategy, an investor sells assets that decline and buys assets that increase in price. This approach's underlying logic is that investors will sell stocks anticipating further decreases if the stock market shows weakness. However, if the market is strong, they will buy stocks expecting continued market gains. Thus, dynamic asset allocation is the opposite of a constant weighting strategy. It's more similar in concept to TAA than SAA.

Constant-weight and dynamic asset allocations have the same advantages and disadvantages. Both strategies are highly flexible in adjusting to market changes and risks. Frequent adjustments to the asset mix can provide higher returns if the investor's decisions are mostly correct. On the other hand, constant rebalancing results in higher transaction costs, lowering a portfolio's overall returns.

- *Insured asset allocation*. This strategy involves establishing a base asset value or floor for the portfolio. As the portfolio value approaches the base value, an investor takes actions to avert further portfolio declines like buying risk-free assets, such as Treasuries, to stabilize the base value. If the portfolio remains above the base value, an investor can engage in active management to increase the portfolio value. An insured asset allocation strategy is appropriate for risk-averse investors who want to engage in active portfolio management and have a specified floor value of a portfolio. This strategy could be attractive to an investor wanting to maintain a minimum standard of living during retirement.
- *Integrated asset allocation*. Integrated asset allocation uses several different asset allocation strategies. It considers an investor's economic expectations and risk in establishing an asset mix. This broader asset allocation strategy excludes combining constant-weighting and dynamic allocation because they're opposites.

In summary, these active management approaches require a high level of knowledge, skill, and research to be successful. Because most individual investors lack these traits, they should avoid using these other asset allocation strategies, especially "do-it-yourself" investors.

What are some guidelines of asset allocation for "average" investors?

The many allocation strategies available to sustainable investors can be confusing. Fortunately, some board consensus exists among investment professionals about the basic guidelines of asset allocation. Below is some advice for "typical" investors.

- *Focus on traditional investments if you're a new or inexperienced investor.* New investors are unlikely to have much knowledge about investing. One of the biggest mistakes they can make is investing in something that they don't understand. However, most investors have heard about stocks, bonds, and cash and cash equivalents, which are traditional investments. Thus, new or inexperienced investors should initially concentrate their asset allocation on such investments before venturing into the area of alternative investments.

- *Increase your allocation to stocks as the time horizon increases.* Individual stocks and overall markets can experience good and bad years. The longer the time horizon, the greater the chance that the good years outweigh the bad ones.

- *Keep some portion of your investment portfolio in stocks regardless of age or risk tolerance.* Including stocks in a portfolio provides diversification and improves total returns over time.

- *Diversify within your portfolio's stock and bond components.* For example, diversifying stocks by size as measured by market capitalization, investment styles such as growth and value, and geographic location can enhance a portfolio's risk–return trade-off. Likewise, diversify bonds in your portfolio by maturity and their types, such as U.S. Treasury, corporate, municipal, agency, and foreign bonds.

- *Emphasize small, growth, and international stocks when you're younger and large-cap stocks and value stocks when you're older.* Younger investors can generally tolerate more risk than older investors due to their longer time horizons.
- *Mix stocks with bonds and cash to moderate portfolio risk.* The returns of stocks, bonds, and cash don't all move together. Thus, portfolio risk decreases by combining traditional asset classes in a portfolio.
- *Shift your portfolio's bond portion from long-term bonds to intermediate-term or short-term bonds as your time horizon shortens.* Shortening the bond maturity leads to more stable bond prices, resulting in lower risk.
- *Increase your portfolio's percentage invested in bonds and cash as your time horizon shortens.* Moving toward assets with more stable prices lowers risk resulting in a more conservative portfolio.

Although these guiding principles primarily apply to "typical investors" for their age, your needs could differ due to your risk tolerance, unique circumstances, and other factors. Thus, you may need to do some tweaking to get a more appropriate asset mix.

What choices are available for determining an asset allocation?

No single asset allocation strategy is best for every investor interested in sustainable investing. The right one depends on your specific situation. The ideal asset allocation is the mix of investments that earn the total return over time you need, given your risk tolerance. Regardless of the strategy chosen, you should feel comfortable that your asset mix provides the best

> "Asset allocation, where you park your money and how you divide it up, is the single most important skill of a successful investor."
> —Tony Robbins

chance of meeting your goals based on a specific risk level. Several ways are available for conscience-based investors to pick an asset allocation. Each option has pros and cons. The following approaches range from customized to standardized.

- *Build your own allocation model.* If you're a reasonably experienced do-it-yourself investor, you can tailor your asset mix to meet your goals within your defined constraints. An excellent choice is to follow an SAA strategy with rebalancing at least annually. As you gain more experience, one of the more complex and nuanced asset allocation strategies may become appealing. However, more active management approaches such as TAA and DAA involve market timing, additional fees, and possible tax payments that "typical" investors usually avoid. However, new or inexperienced investors likely lack the knowledge, skill, and ability to develop an appropriate allocation mix. Therefore, they're better off seeking help with their asset allocations. Fortunately, several avenues are available that can provide such assistance.

- *Use an investment advisor or financial planner.* Various financial professionals are available to assist in working with you to develop a customized asset allocation. The wealthiest investors generally prefer a human advisor. The chief drawback is the cost involved in using an investment advisor or financial planner. Human investment advisors often charge 1% to 2% of your portfolio's value every year. However, not all financial-advisory alternatives require hefty fees. For example, the XY Planning Network is the leading organization of fee-only financial advisors focusing on working with Generation X and Generation Y clients (https://www.xyplanning network.com).

- *Use an online asset allocation tool.* Another approach is to use online asset allocation calculators and tools to help you determine an appropriate asset mix. Because each of these tools uses a different set of assumptions, they're likely to result in somewhat different recommendations. Nevertheless, these tools can serve as a starting point for roughly determining your asset mix. Here are several examples of free asset allocation calculators.

  o Advisorkhoj.com provides an asset allocation calculator using four inputs: your age, risk level, time horizon, and market capitalization of stocks (https://www.advisorkhoj.com/tools-and-calculators/asset-allocation).

  o Bankrate.com has an asset allocation calculator designed to help create a balanced portfolio of stocks, bonds, and cash using seven inputs: age, current assets, saving per year, marginal tax rate, income required, risk tolerance, and economic outlook (https://www.bankrate.com/calculators/retirement/asset-allocation.aspx).

  o CalcXML.com provides a calculator to help determine your portfolio allocation based on your responses to 10 questions (https://www.calcxml.com/calculators/inv01).

  o RealDealRetirement.com offers tools, calculators, research, and other resources to help you with all aspects of retirement planning (https://realdealretirement.com/toolsresources/).

  o SmartAsset.com offers an asset allocation calculator that helps you tailor your allocation to stocks, bonds, and cash to align with your risk tolerance: very conservative, conservative, moderate, aggressive, and very aggressive (https://smartasset.com/investing/asset-allocation-calculator#W20O5SjZih). The website also

> "Whether they're right for you or not, robo-advisors could spell the future of investing."
>
> —Simon Chandler

provides a free tool that matches you with up to three advisors who can provide expertise based on your specific goals.

- *Use a robo-advisor.* You can also receive online advice about developing a portfolio through a *robo-advisor.* These automated financial advice tools provide portfolio solutions to meet your needs, including conscience-based investing. After asking investors questions about your risk tolerance, time horizon, and other preferences, these digital platforms then use algorithms to generate recommendations, including asset allocations, using these inputs. Thus, these investment apps can help the average person make basic investment decisions.

On the positive side, robo-advisors are low cost, simple to use, and easily accessible. They also have low minimum balance requirements. They also provide diversification and most automatically rebalance your portfolio. Another advantage of using robo-advisors is that they help you to avoid making emotional investment decisions. Consequently, they have democratized the investing sphere. Robo-advisors often use indexed strategies involving mutual funds and ETFs, which provide high-quality portfolios. Vanguard promotes its Digital Advisor as tailoring automated investing service to your personal goals. It requires $3,000 to enroll, charges about 0.15% of your Digital Advisor balance annually, around $4.50 a year for a $3,000 portfolio, and provides ongoing, automated investment management. In addition, many robo-advisors make specially tailored portfolios appropriate for sustainable investing. Examples include E*TRADE Core Portfolios, Betterment, Stash, Ellevest, Axos Invest, Ally Invest Managed Portfolios, TD Ameritrade Essential Portfolios, Merrill Edge Guided Investing, and Wealthsimple. Thus, robo-advisors offer similar benefits to those interested in sustainable investing as they do for "typical" investors.

Robo-advisors have drawbacks. Using them requires some faith in the technology and a comfort level with online platforms. A digital advisor can't do everything a financial advisor can, such as providing a holistic look at your total wealth. Thus, robo-advisors have limited abilities and aren't comprehensive financial planners. They offer limited personalization, flexibility, and human interaction. For example, you can't select your investments. If you want to develop a personal relationship with a financial advisor, then a robo-advisor is probably not for you. Finally, some robo-advisors are more costly than all-in-one funds like TDFs.

In summary, robo-advisors are best for novice investors who have a lower net worth, are comfortable with technology, and want to take a "set it and forget it" approach to investing.

- *Invest in an asset allocation fund such as a TDF.* If you have relatively little investment knowledge and experience, you'll probably find asset allocation funds particularly useful. Why? These funds are the simplest possible option. All you must do is select a reputable fund such as Vanguard that matches your expected retirement date or asset allocation, and the fund handles the rest. However, funds with the same target date may have different asset allocations, glide paths, expense ratios. Thus, one size doesn't fit all.

How does asset allocation differ from diversification?

Two key concepts in portfolio management are asset allocation and diversification. Although differences exist between these two strategies, they go together because diversification is part of asset allocation. By constructing a portfolio of different assets, you diversify across several asset classes rather than focus on only one. Additionally, the returns of stocks, bonds, and cash haven't historically moved in unison. As previously discussed, asset allocation involves dividing an

"In choosing a portfolio, investors should seek broad diversification, Further, they should understand that equities—and corporate bonds also—involve risk; that markets inevitably fluctuate; and their portfolio should be such that they are willing to ride out the bad as well as the good times."

—Harry Markowitz

"Here is part of the tradeoff with diversification. You must be diversified enough to survive bad times or bad luck so that skill and good process can have the chance to pay off over the long term."

—Joel Greenblatt

investment portfolio among different asset classes, such as stocks, bonds, and cash, to align with your goals and objectives. It refers to the percentage of each asset class in your portfolio. Thus, asset allocation takes an all-encompassing view of the different types of assets in your portfolio. Diversification involves spreading your investments not only across and within asset classes. For example, you have multiple stocks with different characteristics instead of having only one stock in the stock bucket. You could diversify among small-, mid-, and large-cap stocks and foreign and domestic stocks. Diversification also extends to mixing investment styles. Thus, it goes beyond the investments themselves because it can also relate to the composition and strategies of the teams managing your money.

Why should sustainable investors diversify their portfolios?

Portfolio diversification is a critical part of the investing process and a time-tested method for reducing investment risk. Diversifying across and within different asset classes reduces a portfolio's overall risk (volatility) and enhances risk-adjusted returns by limiting exposure to any single asset or risk. However, diversification can't eliminate all risks and doesn't ensure a profit or guarantee against loss. Moreover, because different asset classes and investments don't move in lockstep with one another, diversification enables you to weather the market's ups and downs. Thus, being "diversified" requires choosing assets such that when some are up, others are down. In mathematical terms, this task entails selecting investments that don't have a high correlation with each other.

Proper diversification offers other potential benefits to sustainable investors. It's a fundamental principle of successful long-term investment that can help you achieve your goals. Diversification can also provide peace of mind by offsetting exposure to a single position and reducing the risk of loss. That is, portfolio diversification reduces the consequences of a wrong forecast by increasing exposure to other opportunities. Through diversification, you can achieve smoother, more consistent investment returns over the medium to long term because no investment consistently outperforms other investments. When investing, there's no such thing as a sure thing. The future is uncertain. By diversifying your portfolio, you're not betting on which horse will win the race. Instead, you're betting on several horses. A final benefit of diversification is that it can lessen the time spent monitoring your portfolio because it's more stable.

What pitfalls involving portfolio diversification should sustainable investors avoid?

Despite the many benefits of diversification, determining the right level of diversification can be difficult. No standardized solution is suitable for all investors. How many stocks or other financial issues can best be included in the portfolio varies based on the individual investor's needs. Thus, each investor needs to find the appropriate balance to achieve a well-diversified portfolio. Allocating funds to different asset classes is a starting point for diversifying a portfolio. The next step is to diversify within each asset class. Like Goldilocks in the story of Goldilocks and the three bears, investors should strive for something that is "just right" for them. In conclusion, diversification is like eating chocolate: it's good but only in moderation.

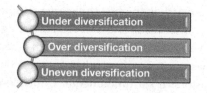

Figure 6.5 The Pitfalls of Diversification

Figure 6.5 shows the three major pitfalls that investors face diversifying their investment portfolios: (1) under diversification, (2) over diversification, and (3) uneven diversification.

- **Under diversification.** With under diversification, investors put their money in a single asset class or hold too few investments in an asset class, such as stocks. Consequently, they may suffer losses if the market turns against a concentrated position and miss out on gains by not having exposure to other well-performing investments. By spreading money across different asset classes and investments, gains from some investments offset losses from others. Thus, a "typical" investor's portfolio should include traditional assets—stocks (equities), bonds and fixed-income securities, and cash and cash equivalents. Failing to look beyond traditional assets to alternative asset classes, if appropriate, is also a form of under diversification.

    Under diversification tends to be greater among younger, low-income, less educated, and less sophisticated investors. Such investors should protect themselves from the dangers of inadequate diversification. Although under diversification is costly to most investors, some highly knowledgeable and experienced investors under diversify by following a

> "As a result of overdiversification, their (active managers) returns get watered down. Diversification covers up ignorance."
>
> —Bill Ackman

focused portfolio strategy. Whatever investment strategy you follow, you should be sure that you know what you're doing.

- **Over diversification.** Another diversification pitfall is *over diversification*, which involves owning too many similar investments. Over diversification can lead to confusion, increased costs, and a complicated tax situation. It can also lead to *diworsification*, which is the process of adding investments to a portfolio that results in a weaker-than-expected risk-adjusted return. One sign of over diversification is owning too many of the same or similar types of securities, mutual funds, or ETFs within your portfolio. This type of investment incurs additional costs or fees without any added diversification.

- **Uneven diversification.** A final diversification pitfall is shifting allocations in one or more asset classes. This situation usually arises when investors fail to rebalance their portfolios. *Rebalancing* is the process of realigning the weightings of your portfolio's asset classes. Although you may start with a target or desired asset allocation, it can get out of balance over time. For example, suppose the stocks in your portfolio enjoy an increase because of a rising stock market. Over time, the value of this asset class could exceed your target percentage and increase your portfolio's overall riskiness. Other asset classes, such as bonds, could diverge from their target proportions. In that case, you should periodically buy or sell assets in your portfolio to maintain an original or desired asset allocation level or risk. Remember that diversification isn't a one-time exercise and requires periodic attention.

How can investors incorporate sustainability into their portfolios?

Below are guidelines for a "typical" investor interested in sustainable investing.

- *Learn the basics of sustainable investing.* A costly mistake that some investors make is investing in something don't understand. Although sustainable investing is not "rocket science," you still need to have sufficient knowledge, skill, and ability to avoid making uninformed decisions resulting in costly mistakes.
- *Decide if you want to be a do-it-yourself investor or if you need professional help.* If you're going to be a DIY investor, you need to do your homework to succeed. If you're unwilling to invest in yourself to learn about sustainable investing, you're better off leaving this take to a trusted advisor or professional money manager. Most individual investors choose the second route.
- *Define what sustainable investing means to you.* Sustainable investing means different things to different people. Clarifying what sustainable investing means to you is critical in aligning your investment goals and personal values. For example, decide what ESG criteria are most important to you. Are you concerned with E or S or G, or with some combination? However, isolating the E from the S and G can sometimes be challenging.
- *Develop a sustainability budget.* Another task is determining how much sustainability you want to incorporate into your overall assets. That is, where do you want to be along the sustainability spectrum from 0% sustainable to 100% sustainable? You can develop a *sustainability budget* indicating the percentage of your portfolio's capital to allocate to sustainable assets. This percentage determines whether sustainability represents a core or satellite component of your portfolio. As the percentage of sustainable assets increases along the sustainability spectrum, so do the time, expertise, and commitment required to manage these assets. Additionally, finding sustainable options across all potential asset classes can be difficult. You also need to decide if you want all or just some of your asset classes to contain sustainable investments.

- *Explore sustainable investment strategies, funds, products, and companies.* Next, you need to determine how to implement sustainability. As discussed in Chapter 4, you have many strategies available to include sustainable investments into your portfolio: (1) screening, (2) ESG integration, (3) socially responsible investing (SRI), (4) shareholder engagement and activism, (5) thematic investing, and (6) impact investing. However, most typical investors often use one of the first three approaches. The screening approach follows a narrow path compared to ESG integration and SRI approaches, which take a more broad-based path.
- *Act and start investing after aligning your goals and values.* For example, suppose your sustainability objective is "do no harm." You may use negative screening to avoid companies or industries whose products conflict with your goals, morals, and values. This simple approach enables you to exclude "sin stocks" and companies engaged in the weapons, alcohol, gambling, or tobacco sectors. You can also select mutual funds and ETFs that filter out specific companies or industries. On the other hand, if you want to invest in companies that "do good," ESG ratings can help you choose individual stocks and funds that align with your goals and values.

  Suppose that your sustainability interests focus on specific themes such as climate change. For example, Invesco WilderHill Clean Energy ETF (PBW) invests in firms that focus on green and renewable energy sources. VanEck Vectors Green Bond ETF (GRNB) invests in green bonds. Others are diversified funds with a sustainable leaning, such as IShares MSCI ACWI Low Carbon Target ETF (CRBN), which gives attention to companies with lower carbon emissions. Still others concentrate on furthering such causes as gender equality (SPDR® SSGA Gender Diversity Index ETF (SHE)) and clean water (Fidelity Water Sustainability Fund (FLOWX)).

- *Review your goals, investment plan, and actions periodically.* Over time, things change, such as your circumstances, the economy, and the market. Consequently, you need to regularly review your goals, investment plan, and actions to ensure they're still appropriate.
- *Make any necessary adjustments.* When needed, you should make necessary changes and base your decisions on sound analysis, not emotions. For example, one adjustment is to rebalance your portfolio to manage your risk and help you stay on track to meet your long-term goals.
- *Stay informed and engaged.* Portfolio management is a continuous process. Whether you're a DIY investor or rely on professional money managers to handle your portfolio, you need to know what's happening with your portfolio.

Why should sustainable investors regularly monitor their portfolios?

Let's face it: things happen that can affect investment portfolios. Some, like market volatility, are expected, while others, like lifestyle changes and pandemics, aren't. Given that life is filled with changes, you need to monitor your portfolio for several reasons. First, you want to ensure that your portfolio adapts to these changes and is aligned to meet your long-term goals. However, achieving your goals isn't always a linear process. You'll encounter ups and downs that you'll need to address. Second, routine monitoring can help identify any holdings that may be failing to meet expectations. You may decide to cut your losses and move into more promising investments. However, you want to base your decisions on sound analysis, not emotions. Third, the portfolio construction process is

"The process of measuring the performance and monitoring the progress of the portfolio as well as the subsequent actions to fine tune the portfolio (if needed) requires an investor to follow a well thought out strategy."

—Hemant Rustogi

ongoing. Making appropriate modifications offers the chance to improve alignment with investment goals. In summary, monitoring your portfolio is one of the keys to investment success.

Should sustainable investors rebalance their portfolios?

If you hold your investments long enough, you're likely to experience *portfolio drift*. That is, your investment mix drifts from your intended asset allocation due to market changes. Rebalancing lets you recalibrate and realign your asset allocation whether the market is up or down. Think about rebalancing as tuning your finances. If you drive a car, it periodically needs maintenance. The same is true for an investment portfolio.

> "Essentially, portfolio rebalancing acts as a tune-up for your investments. It ensures your risk tolerance aligns with your long-term financial goals and gives you a chance to review the types of investments you hold."
>
> —Giovanny Moreano

Suppose your initial allocation is 60% stocks and 40% bonds, but a strong stock market changes the mix to 70%/30%. You can rebalance by selling your high performers (stocks) and reinvesting that money into lower performers (bonds). Thus, you're replacing overweighted assets with underweighted ones. This approach may seem counterintuitive, but it protects you against market fluctuations. You can also invest more money to change the weightings of your asset classes. For example, you could reinvest any cash dividends from stocks into bonds.

Conventional wisdom suggests that regular rebalancing is a sound practice. Yet, some view rebalancing as unnecessary and potentially a mistake. For example, you may not need to rebalance if the portfolio drift is slight. Additionally, some choose to use a *buy-and-hold approach*, a long-term passive strategy where an investor keeps a relatively stable portfolio over time, despite short-term fluctuations. That is, an investor decides upon an allocation mix and doesn't rebalance. This approach tends to perform well in rising markets. Understanding these differing views requires examining the potential benefits and drawbacks of rebalancing.

- *Pros of rebalancing.* On the positive side, rebalancing can control investment risk by keeping your portfolio in line with your risk tolerance and helping you stay on track to meet your long-term goals. Limiting risk is the most apparent benefit of rebalancing. Following a rebalancing strategy can also help you stick to your target allocations and keep your emotions out of your investment decisions, which is typically a good idea. Finally, rebalancing can lead to buying low and selling high, potentially enhancing returns.
- *Cons of rebalancing.* On the downside, rebalancing increases your trading costs and takes time and effort. It's inherently an inefficient tax process resulting in capital gains if you're rebalancing a taxable account. Additionally, rebalancing can lead to missed opportunities if you don't carefully evaluate the circumstances. You wouldn't want to sell a "winner" with solid upside potential or buy a "loser" whose prospects remain bleak for the foreseeable future. Thus, you need to assess a stock's current value and prospects.

If you're a DIY investor, you may view rebalancing as a "pain." However, you have some options. For example, if your portfolio is large enough, you can hire an investment advisor to do it for you for a fee. Other investors can use a robo-advisor like Wealthfront offering rebalancing services or invest in a target-date fund that automatically rebalances. In summary, the pros of rebalancing outweigh the cons. Proper asset allocation is another key to investment success.

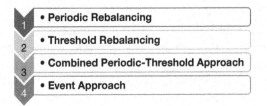

- Periodic Rebalancing
- Threshold Rebalancing
- Combined Periodic-Threshold Approach
- Event Approach

Figure 6.6 Types of Assets Allocation Rebalancing Strategies

What types of asset allocation rebalancing strategies are available, and what are their benefits and drawbacks?

Investors have several rebalancing strategies. The best time and way to rebalance your investment portfolio depends on such factors as your personal preferences, transaction costs, and tax considerations. Figure 6.6 shows several rebalancing options.

- *Periodic rebalancing.* With periodic rebalancing, you establish an ideal allocation within a specified range and periodically rebalance the portfolio to meet this mix. The predetermined dates could be quarterly, semiannually, or annually. Although no magic date exists for rebalancing assets, rebalancing once a year works well for most investors. This strategy works better in markets that tend to rise and fall. However, periodic rebalancing involves commissions, time, and effort. Following this strategy could also result in taxable capital gains.
- *Threshold rebalancing.* Another approach is to rebalance any time your allocation drifts to a certain threshold, either in percent or percentage points. A common rule of thumb is rebalancing the original mix when any asset class moves, say more than 5% or 5 percentage points from its initial value. An advantage of this method is that you buy low and sell high. One drawback is that threshold rebalancing requires more attention.

Additionally, rebalancing costs increase when setting lower thresholds, say 1% or 1 percentage point.

- *Combined periodic-threshold approach.* Using a periodic-threshold approach, you rebalance your portfolio at specific intervals, but only if sufficient drift occurs in the asset allocation, 5% or 5 percentage points. This approach offers a reasonable trade-off between controlling risk and minimizing costs.
- *Event approach.* Another rebalancing strategy involves altering the asset mix after significant market swings.

Of these approaches, using arbitrary dates or thresholds alone to rebalance "robotically" is less effective than either using a combination of the two or events. Preferably, you should time rebalancing for periods when the market trends seem to be reversing because they reflect the most opportune time to rebalance. In addition, owning different asset classes and periodically rebalancing the portfolio to restore the initial allocation between classes reduces overall volatility and ensures a regular harvesting of portfolio gains.

How can sustainable investors evaluate their portfolios?

The last step in the portfolio management process is to analyze your portfolio's performance. Again, it would be best if you made this analysis at least annually. Think of portfolio analysis like your annual medical checkup, except you're looking at your financial health. You may not want to do it, but doing so provides critical feedback on your portfolio, allowing you to adjust and avoid problems. Your portfolio analysis should examine four key areas: (1) performance of individual investments and your portfolio, (2) fees, (3) asset allocation, and (4)

"Without evaluating risk-adjusted returns, an investor cannot possibly see the whole investment picture, which may inadvertently lead to clouded decisions."

—Troy Segal

financial goals. The aim of conducting a portfolio analysis is to determine whether your investment portfolio meets your investing goals and preferences.

Keeping track of your investments can be time-consuming. Fortunately, several approaches are available to simplify your portfolio analysis. One way is to use an online investment analysis tool or software app to manage the process. Two highly rated online platforms are Personal Capital and Morningstar. Quicken Premier offers investment tools to track and analyze a portfolio if you prefer software over an online app. You can set a target asset allocation and Quicken compares it with your portfolio's actual asset allocation. If you don't want to use an online tool or software app, another way to track your investments is to use Google Sheets. However, this approach requires you to enter your portfolio data manually. Of course, if you don't want to do this work yourself, you can get portfolio analysis with a full-service broker like Charles Schwab or Fidelity for a fee.

To better understand how online analysis programs can help, let's briefly examine Personal Capital and Morningstar.

- *Personal Capital.* To begin, you need to open an account and link your financial accounts to its platform. Personal Capital offers a free financial dashboard. You can then use its various tools, such as a retirement planner, fee analyzer, and investment checkup. For example, you can gain insights into your investment performance over time relative to other benchmarks and compare your current portfolio allocation with other possible allocations. Such analyses enable you to determine if your investments are on track to meet your goals.
- *Morningstar.* With Morningstar, you input each of your investments into its Portfolio Manager tool, providing information about your portfolio's overall performance. In addition, a feature called Instant X-Ray provides information on your portfolio's asset allocation. It evaluates

your asset allocation and sector weightings, uncovers concentrated positions, and views the stock holdings behind your mutual funds. Some tools in Portfolio manager require a paid membership.

Takeaways

Sustainable investing isn't a buzzword. It's a way that investors can earn financial returns in sync with their values. That is, you can invest globally in companies that align with the causes that are important to you while providing competitive financial returns. Such investments may meet general ESG requirements or focus more narrowly on such areas as lowering carbon emissions, minority empowerment, or gender diversity. Today, ESG factors can have a material financial impact. Thus, ignoring this impact results in an unfinished puzzle. Sustainable investing lets you live out your beliefs while pursuing your investment goals. Portfolios with purpose represent one of the fastest-growing investment segments, and the trend shows no signs of slowing. Below are some key takeaways for sustainable investors from this chapter.

- Take a portfolio perspective when engaging in sustainable investing.
- Follow the steps in the portfolio management process: planning, execution, and feedback.
- Align your financial goals and values.
- Exercise patience to achieve your long-term financial goals.
- Develop a sustainable investing strategy based on your preferences and motivations.
- Use an asset allocation that reflects your goals, risk tolerance, time horizon, return needs, and personal circumstances.
- Use an appropriate amount of diversification.
- Make monitoring, evaluation, and rebalancing your portfolio a habit.

CHAPTER 5 REFERENCES

Adler, Timothy, and Mark Kritzman. 2008. "The Cost of Socially Responsible Investing." *Journal of Portfolio Management* 35:1, 52–56.

Armstrong, Robert. 2020. "The Fallacy of ESG Investing." October 23. *Financial Times*. Available at https://www.ft.com/content/9e3e1 d8b-bf9f-4d8c-baee-0b25c3113319.

Baker, Malcolm, Daniel Bergstresser, George Serafeim, and Jeff Wurgler. 2018. "Finance the Response to Climate Change: The Pricing and Ownership of U.S. Green Bonds." October 12. Working Paper. National Bureau of Economic Research (NBER). Available at https://papers.ssrn.com/sol3/papers.cfm?abstract_id=3275327.

Barclays. 2016. "Sustainable Investing and Bond Returns." November 1. Barclays. Available at https://www.investmentbank.barclays.com/ content/dam/barclaysmicrosites/ibpublic/documents/our-insig hts/esg/barclays-sustainable-investing-and-bond-returns-3.6mb.pdf.

Barth, Florian, Benjamin Hübel, and Hendrik Scholz. 2021. "ESG and Corporate Credit Spreads." March 21. Working Paper. Friedrich-Alexander-Universität (FAU) Erlangen-Nürnberg. Available at https://papers.ssrn.com/sol3/papers.cfm?abstract_id=3179468.

Bauer, Rob, and Daniel Hann. 2014. "Corporate Environmental Management and Credit Risk." June 25. Working Paper, European Centre for Corporate Engagement (ECCE), Maastricht University. Available at https://papers.ssrn.com/sol3/papers.cfm?abstract_ id=1660470.

Bauer, Rob, Kees Koedijk, and Rogér Otten. 2005. "International Evidence on Ethical Mutual Fund Performance and Investment Style." *Journal of Banking and Finance* 29:1, 1751–1767.

Bauer, Rob, Roger Otten, and Alireza Rad. 2006. "Ethical Investing in Australia: Is There a Financial Penalty?" *Pacific-Basin Finance Journal* 14:1, 33–48.

Blitz, David, and Laurens Swinkels. 2020. "Do Tobacco Share Owners Finance the Tobacco Business?" August 7. Working Paper. Robecco Quantitative Investments. Available at https://papers.ssrn.com/sol3/papers.cfm?abstract_id=3602316.

Bolton, Patrick, and Marcin Kacperczyk. 2021. "Do Investors Care about Carbon Risk?" *Journal of Financial Economics*. Available at https://papers.ssrn.com/sol3/papers.cfm?abstract_id=3398441.

Boubaker, Sabri, Alexis Cellier, Riadh Manita, and Asif Saeed. 2020. "Does Corporate Social Responsibility Reduce Financial Distress Risk?" *Economic Modeling* 91:C, 835–851.

Camejo. Peter. 2002. *The SRI Advantage: Why Socially Responsible Investing Has Outperformed Financially*. Gabriola Island, BC, Canada: New Society.

Capelle-Blancard, Gunther, and Stèphanie Monjon. 2014. "Performance of Socially Responsible Funds: Does the Screening Process Matter?" *European Financial Management* 20:3, 494–520.

Cerulli. 2020. "US ESG Report 2020." Cerulli Associates. Available at https://info.cerulli.com/US-ESG-Report-2020.html.

Chava, Sudheer. 2014. "Environmental Externalities and Cost of Capital." June 18. Working Paper. Georgia Institute of Technology. Available at https://papers.ssrn.com/sol3/papers.cfm?abstract_id=1677653.

Clark, Gordon, Andreas Feiner, and Michael Viehs. 2015. "From the Stockholder to the Stakeholder: How Sustainability Can Drive Financial Outperformance." March 6. Arabesque Partners and the University of Oxford. Available at https://papers.ssrn.com/sol3/papers.cfm?abstract_id=2508281.

Cohen, Lauren, Umit Gurun, and Quoc Nguyen, 2021. "The ESF-Innovation Disconnect: Evidence from Green Patenting." March 30. Working Paper, National Bureau of Economic Research (NBER). Available at https://papers.ssrn.com/sol3/papers.cfm?abstract_id=3718682.

Counts, Cecelie. 2013. "Divestment Was Just One Weapon in Battle Against Apartheid." January 26. *The New York Times*. Available at https://www.nytimes.com/roomfordebate/2013/01/27/is-divestment-an-effective-means-of-protest/divestment-was-just-one-weapon-in-battle-against-apartheid.

Davies, Shaun, and Edward Van Wesep. 2018. "The Unintended Consequences of Divestment." *Journal of Financial Economics* 128:3, 558–575.

Derwall, Jeroen, Nadja Guenster, Rob Bauer, and Kees G. Koedijk. 2005. "The Eco-Efficiency Premium Puzzle." *Financial Analysts Journal* 61:2, 51–63.

Derwall, Jeroen, and Kees Koedijk. 2009. "Socially Responsible Fixed-Income Funds." *Journal of Business Finance and Accounting* 36:1–2, 210–229.

DiBartolomeo, Dan. 2010. "Equity Risk, Credit Risk, Default Correlation and Corporate Sustainability." *Journal of Investing* 19:4, 128–133.

DiBartolomeo, Dan, and Lloyd Kurtz. 1999. "Managing Risk Exposures of Socially Screened Accounts." September 9. Working Paper, Northfield Information Services. Available at https://www.tias.edu/docs/default-source/documentlibrary_fsinsight/research-paper-dibartolomeo-kurtz-1999.pdf.

DiBartolomeo, Dan, and Lloyd Kurtz. 2011. "The Long-Term Performance of a Social Investment Universe." *Journal of Investing* 20:3, 95–102.

EY. 2020. "Global Alternative Fund Survey." Ernst & Young (EY). Available at https://www.researchgate.net/publication/23724220_Do_Corporate_Global_Environmental_Standards_in_Emerging_Markets_Create_Or_Destroy_Market_Value.

Fabozzi, Frank J., K. C. Ma, and Becky J. Oliphant. 2008. "Sin Stock Returns." *Journal of Portfolio Management* 35:1, 82–94.

Ferrell, Allen, Liang Hao, and Luc Renneboog. 2016. "Socially Responsible Firms." *Journal of Financial Economics* 122:3, 585–606.

Flammer, Caroline. 2021. "Corporate Green Bonds." *Journal of Financial Economics.* 142:2, 499–516.

Fossil Free. 2021. "1200+ Divestment Commitments." GoFossilFree.org. Available at https://gofossilfree.org/divestment/commitments.

Fulton, Mark, Bruce Kahn, and Camilla Sharples. 2012. "Sustainable Investing: Establishing Long-Term Value and Performance." June 12. Working Paper. Deutsche Bank and Columbia University. Available at https://papers.ssrn.com/sol3/papers.cfm?abstract_id=2222740.

Gantchev, Nickolay, Mariassunta Giannetti, and Rachel Li. 2021. "Sustainability or Performance? Ratings and Fund Managers' Incentives." June 8. Working Paper, Centre for Economic Policy Research (CEPR), European Corporate Governance Institute

(ECGI). Available at https://papers.ssrn.com/sol3/papers.
cfm?abstract_id=3731006.

Geczy, Christopher C., Robert F. Stambaugh, and David Levin. 2005.
"Investing in Socially Responsible Mutual Funds." October.
Working Paper. The Rodney L. White Center of Financial Research
and Wharton School, University of Pennsylvania. Available at
https://repository.upenn.edu/cgi/viewcontent.cgi?article=
1444&context=fnce_papers.

Gompers, Paul, Joy L. Ishii, and Andrew Metrick. 2001. "Corporate
Governance and Equity Prices." *Quarterly Journal of Economics* 118:1,
107–155.

Goss, Allen. 2007. "Corporate Social Responsibility and Financial
Distress." August 1. Working Paper. Ryerson School of Management.
Available at https://www.researchgate.net/publication/255996683_
Corporate_Social_Responsibility_and_Financial_Distress.

Goss, Allen, and Gordon Roberts. 2011. "The Impact of Corporate Social
Responsibility on the Cost of Bank Loans." *Journal of Banking and
Finance* 35:7, 1794–1810.

Guenster, Nadja, Rob Bauer, Jeroen Derwall, and Kees Koedijk. 2011.
"The Economic Value of Corporate Eco-Efficiency." *European
Financial Management* 17:4, 679–704.

Guerard, John B., Jr. 1997. "Is There a Cost to Being Socially Responsible
in Investing?" *Journal of Investing* 6:2, 11–18.

Gurun, Umit, Jordan Nickerson, and David Solomon. 2020. "The Perils
of Private Provision of Public Goods." October 12. Working Paper.
Available at https://papers.ssrn.com/sol3/papers.cfm?abstract_
id=3531171.

Hale, Jon. 2020. "The Sustainable Funds Landscape in 6 Charts."
Morningstar. March 18. Available at https://www.morningstar.
com/insights/2020/03/18/sustainable-funds-in-6-charts.

Hale, Jon. 2021. "A Broken Record: Flows for U.S. Sustainable Funds
Again Reach New Heights." January 18. Morningstar. Available at
https://www.morningstar.com/articles/1019195/a-broken-record-
flows-for-us-sustainable-funds-again-reach-new-heights.

Hamilton, Sally, Hoje Jo, and Meir Statman. 1993. "Doing Well While
Doing Good? The Investment Performance of Socially Responsible
Mutual Funds." *Financial Analysts Journal* 49:6, 62–66.

Hong, Harrison, and Marcin Kacperczyk. 2009. "The Price of Sin: The
Effects of Social Norms on Markets." *Journal of Financial Economics*
93:1, 15–36.

Huang, Nellie. 2021. "How Green Are Your Bonds?" February 23. *Kiplinger*. Available at https://www.kiplinger.com/investing/mutual-funds/602283/how-green-are-your-bonds.

Iacurci, Greg. 2020. "Climate Funds Hold Less than 1% of 401(k) Money. Here's Why." December 14. CNBC. Available at https://www.cnbc.com/2020/12/11/heres-why-401k-plans-lag-in-green-investment-options.html.

Jin, Henry H., Olivia S. Mitchell, and John Piggott. 2006. "Socially Responsible Investment in Japanese Pensions." *Pacific-Basin Journal* 14:5, 427–438.

Kempf, Alexander, and Peer Osthoff. 2008. "SRI Funds: Nomen Est Omen." *Journal of Business Finance and Accounting* 35:9–10, 1276–1294.

Kim, Irene, and Mohan Venkatachalam. 2011. "Are Sin Stocks Paying the Price for Accounting Sins?" *Journal of Accounting, Auditing, and Finance* 26:2, 415–442.

Kreander, Niklas, Rob Gray, David Power, and C. D. Sinclair. 2002. "The Financial Performance of European Ethical Funds 1996–1998." *Journal of Accounting and Finance* 1:January, 3–22.

Kreander, Niklas, Rob Gray, David Power, and C. D. Sinclair. 2005. "Evaluating the Performance of Ethical and Non-Ethical Funds: A Matched Pair Analysis." *Journal of Business Finance and Accounting* 32:7–8, 1465–1493.

Kurtz, Lloyd, and Dan DiBartolomeo. 2005. "The KLD Catholic Values 400 Index." *Journal of Investing* 14:3, 101–104.

Iachini, Michael. 2020. "How Well Has Socially Responsible Investing Performed?" June 25. Charles Schwab. Available at https://www.schwab.com/resource-center/insights/content/how-well-has-socially-responsible-investing-performed.

Larcker, David, and Edward Watts. 2019. "Where's the Greenium?" February 29. Working Paper. Stanford Graduate School of Business. Available at https://www.gsb.stanford.edu/faculty-research/working-papers/wheres-greenium.

Li, Feifel, and Ari Polychronopoulos. 2020. "What a Difference an ESG Ratings Provider Makes." January. Research Affiliates. Available at https://www.researchaffiliates.com/en_us/publications/articles/what-a-difference-an-esg-ratings-provider-makes.html.

Lins, Karl, Henri Servaes, and Ane Tamayo. 2017. "Social Capital, Trust, and Firm Performance: The Value of Corporate Social Responsibility during the Financial Crisis." *Journal of Finance* 72:4, 1785–1824.

Lu, H. Arthur, and Ronald Balvers. 2015. "Social Screens and Systematic Boycott Risk." April 10. Working Paper. McMaster University DeGroote School of Business. Available at https://papers.ssrn.com/sol3/papers.cfm?abstract_id=2474255.

Managi, Shunsuke, Tatsuyoshi Okimoto, and Akimi Matsuda. 2012. "Do Socially Responsible Investment Indexes Outperform Conventional Indexes?" *Applied Financial Economics* 22:18, 1511–1527.

Mize, Geoffrey, Elyse Reilly, and Andre Veissed. 2021. "Why Asset Managers Look at Divestments in Response to Market Challenges." May 25. Ernst & Young. Available at https://www.ey.com/en_us/divestment-study/wealth-asset-management.

Morgan Stanley. 2019. "Sustainable Reality: Analyzing Risk and Returns of Sustainable Funds." Morgan Stanley Institute for Sustainable Investing. Available at https://www.morganstanley.com/pub/content/dam/msdotcom/ideas/sustainable-investing-offers-financial-performance-lowered-risk/Sustainable_Reality_Analyzing_Risk_and_Returns_of_Sustainable_Funds.pdf.

Morgan Stanley. 2020a. "Sustainable Signals: Asset Owners See Sustainability as Core to the Future of Investing." Morgan Stanley Institute for Sustainable Investing. Available at: https://www.morganstanley.com/content/dam/msdotcom/sustainability/20-05-22_3094389%20Sustainable%20Signals%20Asset%20Owners_FINAL.pdf.

Morgan Stanley. 2020b. "Sustainable Reality: 2020 Update." Morgan Stanley Institute for Sustainable Investing. Available at https://www.morganstanley.com/content/dam/msdotcom/en/assets/pdfs/3190436-20-09-15_Sustainable-Reality-2020-update_Final-Revised.pdf.

Morgan Stanley. 2020c. "Sustainable Funds Outperform Peers in 2020 during Coronavirus." February 24. Morgan Stanley Institute for Sustainable Investing. Available at https://www.morganstanley.com/ideas/esg-funds-outperform-peers-coronavirus.

Morningstar. 2021. "Sustainable Funds U.S. Landscape Report: More Funds, More Flows, and Impressive Returns in 2020." February 10. Morningstar. Available at https://www.morningstar.com/lp/sustainable-funds-landscape-report.

MSCI. 2020. "ESG Ratings: Measuring a Company's Resilience to Long-term, Financially Relevant ESG Risks." October. MSCI. Available at https://www.msci.com/our-solutions/esg-investing/esg-ratings.

MSCI. 2021. "MSCI KLD 400 Social Index (USD)." MSCI. Available at https://www.msci.com/documents/10199/904492e6-527e-4d64-9904-c710bf1533c6.

O'Brien, Amy, Lei Liao, and Jim Campagna. 2018. "Responsible Investing: Delivering Competitive Performance." Summer. Nuveen TIAA Investments. Available at https://www.tiaa.org/public/pdf/delivering_competitive_performance.pdf.

Orlitzky, Marc, Frank L. Schmidt, and Sara L. Rynes. 2003. "Corporate Social and Financial Performance: A Meta-Analysis." *Organization Studies* 24:3, 403–441.

Painter, Marcus. 2020. "An Inconvenient Cost: The Effects of Climate Change on Municipal Bonds." *Journal of Financial Economics* 135:2, 468–482.

Pástor, Ľuboš, Robert Stambaugh, and Lucian Taylor. 2021. "Sustainable Investing in Equilibrium." *Journal of Financial Economics* 142:2, 550–571.

Pedersen, Lasse, Shaun Fitzgibbons, and Lukasz Pomorski. 2021. "Responsible Investing: The ESG-efficient Frontier." *Journal of Financial Economics* 142:2, 572–597.

Renneboog, Luc, Jenke Ter Horst, and Chendi Zhang. 2008a. "Socially Responsible Investments: Institutional Aspects, Performance, and Investor Behavior." *Journal of Banking and Finance* 32:1, 1723–1742.

Renneboog, Luc, Jenke Ter Horst, and Chendi Zhang. 2008b. "The Price of Ethics and Stakeholder Governance: The Performance of Socially Responsible Mutual Funds." *Journal of Corporate Finance* 14:1, 302–322.

Schröder, Michael. 2004. "The Performance of Socially Responsible Investments: Investment Funds and Indices." *Financial Markets and Portfolio Management* 18:2, 122–142.

Schröder, Michael. 2007. "Is There a Difference? The Performance Characteristics of SRI Equity Indices." *Journal of Business Finance & Accounting* 34:1–2, 331–348.

SIF. 2020. "Report on US Sustainable and Impact Investing Trends 2020." Social Investment Forum (SIF). Available at https://www.ussif.org/files/Trends%20Report%202020%20Executive%20Summary.pdf.

Statman, Meir. 2000. "Socially Responsible Mutual Funds." *Financial Analysts Journal* 56:3, 30–39.

Statman, Meir. 2006. "Socially Responsible Indexes: Composition, Performance, and Tracking Error." *Journal of Portfolio Management* 32:3, 100–109.

Statman, Meir, and Denys Glushkov. 2009. "The Wages of Social Responsibility." *Financial Analysts Journal* 65:4, 33–46.

Stevens, Pippa. 2019. "Your Complete Guide to Investing with a Conscience, a $30 Trillion Market Just Getting Started." December 16. CNBC. Available at https://www.cnbc.com/2019/12/14/your-complete-guide-to-socially-responsible-investing.html.

Teoh, Siew H., Ivo Welch, and C. Paul Wazzan. 1999. "The Effect of Socially Activist Investment Policies on the Financial Markets: Evidence from the South African Boycott." *Journal of Business* 72:1, 35–89.

UN. 2020. "The Sustainable Development Goals Report." United Nations (UN). Available at https://unstats.un.org/sdgs/report/2020.

Whelan, Tensie, Ulrich Atz, Tracy Van Hold, and Casey Clark. 2020. "ESG and Financial Performance: Uncovering the Relationship by Aggregating Evidence from 1,000 Plus Studies Published between 2015–2020." NYU Stern Center for Sustainable Business and Rockefeller Asset Management. Available at https://www.stern.nyu.edu/sites/default/files/assets/documents/NYU-RAM_ESG-Paper_2021%20Rev_0.pdf.

INDEX

Tables and figures are indicated by *t* and *f* following the page number.